## Contents

## Editor's Introduction

These fabricated essays present the essential teaching of nine teachers whose insights helped shape my understanding of and relationship with the Divine Presence. Each essay reconstructs the approach taken by that teacher to reveal personal, first-hand understanding of the God-self relationship. Each makes clear how to see and break through myths about self and return to that point of consciousness where we are at-one with God.

I drew these materials from core writing of each teacher, and reshaped them so they are transparent, provocative, and instructional. The text is presented largely in the second person as teaching directed from the teacher to you, the student. If I found some statement from the original text that was not immediately clear to me, I gently edited it so that I "got it." I took care not to distort the teaching to the extent that it became more mine than theirs.

A basic challenge that is repeated throughout this collection of essays: It is time for you to stop playing mental games and instead awaken to your Self! Each essay goes farther in offering clear instructions for how to make this happen *right now* by shifting the way you know yourself and see the world. The promise of this action is an intimate and authentic relation with God.

The collection does not promote a single viewpoint or philosophy regarding who or what is God, and does not promote a "best" religion or discipline for closing the distance to God. None of these nine individuals make claims to have *the* monopoly on the truth. These five Eastern and four Western teachers approach spiritual inquiry through different disciplines and lenses, yet there is a sense of wholeness and integrity to what they offer collectively. They are each speaking from a root level where unity rather than divisiveness prevails.

Each essay is an invitation to the reader to adopt that teacher for a brief while as a seasoned guide and discover what might be learned from travelling on a mental journey with that guide. They present what they have learned and what has worked for them.

What they teach, if approached with an open mind and heart, can serve to strengthen and mature one's own practices, faith, and connection with God.

The five spiritual guides from the East were among the most popular and respected teachers and mystics of the past century. They played a major role in bringing Eastern spirituality to Europe and North America. The four Westerners echoed these teachings with their own unique spins on Self-consciousness. There is no clash here between East and West. Through the essays, each "side" offers parallel advice on what to stop and what to do (or not-do) so that welcomed results immediately follow.

Each essay is fascinating in its own right. Each reflects the unbridled passion and complete sincerity of that teacher. The advice offered is plausible and compelling, even should you not buy into every single statement. These instructions have been endorsed, in the case of the five teachers from the East, by their multiple thousands of devoted followers.

You can begin with any essay and then freely move across them to find a coherent thread of discourse, advice, and wisdom. My editing aimed at making this feasible. I also made use of several section headings for each essay to allow "essay hopping" around particular themes of interest. The table of contents includes these headings to encourage such cross-essay exploration. Akin to the I Ching, you can also open to any page and paragraph and find immediate wisdom to inform your day.

It is hard to imagine any open-minded and open-hearted individual interested in deepening their spiritual understandings and practice who will not find inspiration and insight in this collection. The nine teachers—while clearly not representative of all faiths and spiritual disciplines—were among the 20th century's best. The nine teachers would definitely be included in a Who's Who of the field.

- Yogi Bhajan, a deeply devoted Sikh, helped hundreds of thousands of individuals to learn meditation and guided many to experience life more fully. He introduced Kundalini yoga practice to the United States and established the first International Peace Prayer Day Celebration.

- Paramahansa Yogananda, an Indian yogi and guru, had a profound influence on thousands of Americans in the first decades of the twentieth century. A half century later, he gained a second audience, when he and his lineage were prominently featured on the cover of the classic Beatle's album, Sergeant Pepper's Lonely Heart Club's Band.

- Ramana Maharshi was considered by insiders as one of the greatest, perhaps the greatest spiritual teacher of modern-day India. His method of self-inquiry cut through philosophical discourse and religious rituals to reach the root question, "Who am I?"

- J. Krishnamurti was dubbed "the teacher of the age" by European theosophists. He rejected the title with its exalted status and instead traveled the globe encouraging audiences to stay totally aware in the present moment and reject all divisions. He boldly claimed that this was the only path to eliminating conflict in one's life and in the world.

- Bhagwan Shree Rajneesh is the maverick in the group. He led an outrageous and controversial life among his community of followers. He wrote brilliant and simultaneously humorous commentaries that spanned a wide range of disciplines and spiritual texts.

- Martin Buber's concept of I-Thou continues to have a major impact on those interested in understanding the spiritual nature of inter-personal and trans-personal relationships. The ever-constant choice to meet the world through either secular I-it encounters or divine I-Thou relations lies at or close to the root of all enlightened psychologies.

- I took a leap and included an essay drawn from the "channeled" messages of Bartholomew as expressed through Mary Margaret Moore, which I personally have found to be very moving in their wisdom and good sense. The advice to "snuggle into the moment" and "to be kind to my cells" has served me well over the years and saved a lot of fruitless searching for truth elsewhere than right here.

- Franklin Merrell-Wolff was a philosopher with an interest in transcended consciousness. He explored a great many spiritual approaches before adopting the Vedanta school of Hindu philosophy, and particularly the ideas expressed by Shankara, as core to his belief. I concluded the essay with his parable of the journey to enlightenment.

- Insights and prophetic musings of Julius Stulman round out and add a different spice to this collection. Julius was my personal teacher and never ceased to impress me with his ability to read the future as though it were already happening and, often, to describe it through poetic verse. He was the publisher of the journal, Main Currents in Modern Thought, an innovative attempt to bridge between modern systems thinkers and traditional Eastern practices. He edited and contributed extensively to a second journal, Fields Within Fields...Within Fields.

For my part in this, I went to the essential writings of each teacher and extracted the statements that I personally found most illuminating and evocative. I did some minor editing to link these statements together as a coherent whole and recapture their voices, and then hopefully got out of the way. Enjoy.

Barry Kibel
Tucson, Arizona

Note about gender. These teachers wrote in a period when "man" was used to refer to both genders. It is clear from their writings that they meant to be gender inclusive. I modified the writing where this occurred to capture both genders. I was initially fearful that the editing in this regard would become too heavy-handed and the flow of the language would get lost. In the end, I dived in and made the changes. Hopefully their insights and universal messages did not get distorted.

# 1
# Yogi Bhajan

*Yogi Bhajan (1929-2004) was the chief religious and administrative authority for the Sikh Dharma in the western hemisphere. He helped hundreds of thousands of individuals to learn meditation and guided many to experience life more fully. The materials presented here were extracted and gently edited from The Teachings of Yogi Bhajan (New York: Hawthorn Books, Inc., 1977).*

## Realizing Yourself

What are you doing on the planet earth? You are here to realize yourself and nothing more. That's it. This opportunity exists for human beings and not in the vegetable or animal world. You have a chance to awaken to your Soul, to be the great discoverer and expression of God-consciousness. In this finite form, the body has been given to you to experience Infinity, to receive love from the Unknown.

This is your purpose: to find and interplay with Infinity, to experience in you the vastness of Infinity. You should not only know this, you should understand it deeply and intimately, beyond words and thoughts. Your basic fundamental existence has this one purpose. Once you awaken, you are all right. And that awakening does not require years of searching outside you. You ***are*** a living existence of infinite Light; you need not seek anything.

The play of life is to inspire each other to God-consciousness. Play your role as gracefully as you can and relax. You are here to remain graceful and face all ungraceful environments with grace. It is a privilege to be allowed to do so. Patience pays. Let no temptation shake you, no vibration move you, and no action force you out of yourself and righteousness. An unshakable human being is the highest living phenomenon of God. It is God who created you and it is *to* God that you will go. Nothing exists in between.

You have forgotten who you are. You are one and there is One to whom you belong. The world is a temporary visitation. Visit it with love. You are here to do something that will live forever. Make your temple clean. Make your heart open with love so that God can come and sit in it.

## The Mystery of God

Most of us do not know what God is and sometimes, for fun's sake, we do not believe in God. God does not send a letter to you saying, "Please recognize Me." When you cannot see the orange tree in the seed, how can you see God in this world? God is the secret eye of the self and is in every self. God is not a phenomenon. God is Infinite, but also finite. God dances with you. God does everything with you.

God is not living on the seventh floor and no elevator goes to Him. There is no distance between you and God; it is your thinking that puts you at a distance. God is you. He is your identity in existence. That is why God is everywhere. Because wherever you are, God is. I assure you, God looks after you and lives through you. Recognize God. You are the manifestation of the Creator.

From morning to evening we want you to meditate on one thought: "There is one Creator who created this universe and that very same God is personified in this universe as me and as you." Do you know that the great Unknown One *is* you? God is not outside. God is not anywhere. God starts as charity starts, right from one's own home. And don't think of him as upstairs. You are God; without God you do not exist.

What is Godhood? When you cannot find your length and breadth, your height and depth—that is Godhood. By God, I mean the infinite Creator, the Giver of energy, and the Power through which our breath fluctuates in us as we inhale and exhale. God doesn't exist because of you; you exist because of God. If you realize that God is omniscient, omnipresent, and omnipotent, then you must forget *finding* God. You have already found God. God is in you and you are in God. If you have no real connection with God in that way, then keep on searching... but I can guarantee that you will never find God in another way.

A human being is a creature, a puppet hung on the string of breath. When you say, *I* can do it or *I* cannot do it, you are fooling yourself. Instead you should say, "As is the Will of the Divine, it is being tried through me. If I am successful, it is God's grace; if not, it is God's Will." God gives me breath to speak and God gives you breath to listen. In essence, there is no difference between me and you. God is speaking and God is listening, and that is "maya." What appears as two is truly the One. If you understand this "maya," you will understand everything.

What is realization? When you become that which you realize. If you realize God, then you become God. God is nothing but Universality in experience. When you experience a Universal consciousness in your finite consciousness—that is what God is all about. Once you have seen Divine everywhere, you cannot see anything else. Your sight has taken you beyond time, beyond karmas.

"I am" is not a complete mantra. It must be, "I am, I am." "I am" is the Infinite and "I am" is the finite. The mind must shuttle freely between the two. We have not realized in our finite selves our Infinite origin and destiny. We relate to our limitedness. We have not realized in ourselves our total Potency.

Between you and God there is no difference. The difference is in the realization. You may not have realized that you are God, you might keep insisting that you are merely human. You are failing to realize that there is an Infinite being inside you. Your Source is beyond finiteness. And what is this beyond point? Call it God, call it Buddha, or call it anything you choose. God is a realization.

## Getting Out of Your Own Way

The limited mental self and the unlimited higher Self exist in apparent opposition, but must be reconciled. Whether your limited mind relates to it or not, you are not only or fundamentally that mind. You are also that which is *beyond* that mind. If you cannot recognize the fight in you between these two selves, then you know absolutely nothing about yourself. But gradually you will realize this conflict within you, and you will be able to overcome that conflict so that the higher Self may win.

A person is limited according to his attachment to the mental self and to the things and ideas it possesses. It doesn't matter what you have or don't have; it matters only how easily you can let go of these limitations. When unlimited life is lived, everything comes to you. But when a limited you lives life, then you have to struggle for everything. Life is a Limitless game, but the limited self does not want to play unattached and unlimited. It chooses to play for the sake of limited wins and losses, and that is where unhappiness ultimately comes in. Sooner or later, limited life does not feel quite right or authentic.

The mind is like a mirror through which you can see Infinity. But if you put blackness over it, you will see nothing. What use is a mirror in which you cannot see yourself? When you have a desire and it is not satisfied... that produces blackness. It does not matter what the desire is. When you keep negativity within yourself—that produces blackness. If your inner world is disturbed, your outer world also become disturbed and you see the whole world around you as disturbed. That produces blackness.

You make habits and then habits make you. If you have any habit, you will be a slave of that habit. This is your slavery. Liberation is the state beyond habits. Don't let the mind lead you to form habits or you will not be able to see beyond it and will end up a slave to it. The mind is given to you to serve you, not enslave you. You must be its guide and keep it unencumbered. Only a relaxed and unencumbered mind will bring you the realization of God-consciousness.

You are related to the universe through your mind. The moment you *also* relate to your Soul, your mind becomes your servant. If you train yourself that you are limited, everything is limited for you and you become the slave. When you train your mind to understand that you are Unlimited, then every bounty for you is Unlimited. Then, the whole of nature serves you.

You are a part of the universe and the universe is a part of you. It is a simple thing. When you are attached to a limited mind, how can you be Universal? How can you be Infinite? You have to be you, but you can only be you when you understand that you are part of Infinity.

At heart, no one wants to become limited, because the source of each one is Infinite. The Creator created the creature to realize the finite of the Infinite. The moment you feel that, while finite, you are part of Infinity and that Infinity is part of you, your limitations will cease and happiness will flow. When you can imagine in action or inaction that you belong to Infinity, then you are beautiful.

## Know Thyself

Your end is Infinity. Your beginning is Infinity. You are only in trouble when you have not realized you are Infinity. To realize the Infinity in the finite state is the challenge and the opportunity of the mind. The purpose of finite knowledge is to develop Infinite faith in self. When you say, "I am a God-conscious person," it means you realize that your mental capacity is Infinite. You realize that your mind is the link between your existence reality and *your* total Infinity.

When the little "me" has recognized the big "Me" and the little "i" has recognized the big "I", oneness is achieved. And when one knows that he is the One and one knows everything is One, then what is there to find? It is only when you think that "I am" *and* "everything else is everything else" that you have to find something. If you can sacrifice your limited ego, you will always get in return an unlimited Spirit.

You don't need to be spiritual, you need not be holy, and you need not study under a great master. You aren't required to follow anybody, you aren't required to be with anybody, you aren't required to learn anything, if—it's a big if—*if* you know who you are, and not only know, but *realize* who you are. The moment you meet a man or woman of God-consciousness, they will tell you, "Know Thyself." The inner Self of the self is sitting, waiting for you to *realize* your existence.

Many people think you have to seek approval from others or from God. All you have to do is approve of yourself. The amount of happiness that lies within you depends on how open, how positive, and how accurately righteous you are. This is the secret of happiness. If you want to be great, then you will have to feel great and act great.

If you want to be Godly, you have to feel and act Godly. Be creative, be loving, be giving, be great, and God will give you bounty. There will be no limit. Whatever you plant in the spring, it will grow. So, if in your own ecology you will sprout positivity, service, smiles, charm, happiness, and good faith, you will grow and you will be unlimited. You will be content. You will be grateful to be alive.

To recognize the "truth," first recognize that you *are* the Truth. You belong to only one thing, and that is Truth; and you have got to be delivered to only one thing, and that is Truth. You are true now, you were true then, and you shall ever be true–that is all you have to know, and you will be free.

If you want to experience the Infinite consciousness, which is God, you can only experience that through the Self. You don't have to aim to realize God and you don't have to aim to realize Infinity. All you have to do is realize the Truth of your existence. Your existence is nothing but Infinite Consciousness. If your existence is nothing but Consciousness, where is the difficulty?

The difficulty is that you are not conscious of your Infinite Consciousness. When you trust your greatness, you will always be great. Trust itself is Self-realization. "I am, I am" is the ultimate declaration of trust, and when this idea is perceived, nothing else is required.

The fundamental truth is to realize, to feel, and to experience Infinite life within you. We normally experience feel and experience limited life within us in relationship to environments; so we feel environments, not life. One who experiences life, experiences the Source of life. One who experiences the Source of life, knows Infinity.

When you know that all is Light, then you are enlightened. What is enlightenment? When you recognize the Light. Where? Within you. Behave so as to maintain the flame of Light to the end; your karma will be done, blessings will exist, awareness will be the gift. That is the rightful right of every person. That is the Truth in you. When you live the Truth, you become the Truth.

The human being is limited because the human being has never experienced one's own Self. The moment you become aware of who you are, everyone on this planet will become aware of who you are. Your only setback is when you are not aware of who you are.

You see yourself as only one thing, a limited thing, but you are *everything* all the time, under all circumstances. Your power lies in the fact that the entire universe, in a mini-form of the vaster universe, rotates in and around you. Your micro-consciousness vibrates with, and is essentially one with, the macro-Consciousness. To understand the former is to understand the latter. The moment you become aware of the unlimited Self, your frequency changes and the universe around you changes also. This is a cosmic law.

The "mud of time" is a state of mind in which a person, over Universal consciousness, gives preference to finite matters and physical materials. Get out of the mud! Have faith in yourself because you are an unlimited Self. You are Immortal. You are a Divine consciousness. Nothing is beyond the Self, nothing was beyond the Self, and nothing shall be beyond the Self. You are an unlimited Self in the beginning and an unlimited Self in the end. Once you realize the unlimited Self, you will be a realized Self.

### Meditation

All teachings, whether they were taught in the past or whether they are taught now or whether they will be taught in the coming generations, have one idea alone, and the only idea is to make people realize God consciously. The secret of all teachings, all masters, all gurus, all messengers, all messiahs, is one–that at any stage, under any circumstances, people have the power to convert themselves into Super-human beings by consciously realizing the supreme Godhead.

To realize God, you must empty yourself and let the universe come in you. This is meditation. The aim is to become nothing, so that *everything* can flow through you. Meditation is a mental cleansing. Good meditation is when all the garbage comes out. What remains is individual harmony that exists in relationship to universal Harmony. When the one-pointed, infinite beam of the mind starts sending the signal into the Infinity and the Infinity relates to the finite, union occurs.

The mantra I teach is Sa-Ta-Na-Ma. Sat Nam means Truth manifested. By vibrating in rhythm with the breath to that sound, Sa-Ta-Na-Ma, you can expand your sensitivity to the entire spectrum of vibration. It is similar to striking a note on a stringed instrument. As you vibrate, the universe vibrates with you. Draw from the universe that great energy and feel it in every cell of your body. Let every cell of your body vibrate and extend that vibration to every extent. Feel it as a big whirlwind of energy circling with each cell of your body. Just concentrate and feel it in you.

To be calm is the highest achievement of the self. The active mind becomes still when you meditate, and the passive mind becomes active. When thoughts come to you, don't get upset; let them pass through. And when they pass through, just sit and laugh that they are gone. Feel relaxed. After some time of meditation, you will find a time when no thought will be released by the passive mind. Then you will enjoy a state of bliss. You will recognize the one true Reality: you breathe in and you breathe out. That is it.

Levitate your consciousness to total nothingness: "I was not, I am not, and I shall be not." Do not let your mind betray you, because your mind and your Soul must at this time unite together. Meditation is the creative control of the self where the Infinite can talk to you. A relaxed mind is a creative mind and a creative mind is a relaxed mind. Only a relaxed mind can become a one-pointed mind, and a one-pointed mind is the most wonderful mind. It is the most powerful, it can do anything. Universal realization comes when you see yourself as nothing but a Point. As a Point, you do not know how you exist, but still you *are* existing, and this is the wonder of reality.

## Spiritual Teachers and Gurus

When there is an end to a search, you have found. So long as there is a search, you are searching. "Where to end the search?" is the question. End the search where you meet a person of faith. Who is a person of faith? The first sign of a saint is that she or he is original. She *is* what she *is*. He *is* what he *is*. Then, talk to that person on any facet; if through every talk you are shown the path of God, you have found the right person. As you talk, you will hear the language of Infinity. In the end, you will be led to one thing: that the total creation is created by the Creator and you are part of that Infinity.

Spiritual teaching is not a verbalization or a communication; spiritual teaching is also not a direction. Spiritual teaching is to *be.* The job of the teacher is not to teach you the Truth, because you know the Truth... You know the Truth. The job of the teacher is, out of her or his practical life and experience, to remind you to *live* the Truth. That's all it is. There is nothing which you do not know. A teacher is a reminder. The teacher gives you something to focus on to help you find the Infinite, to remind you that you belong in the finite to the Infinite. The relationship between the student and teacher is firmly established at that stage when the student realizes the ecstasy of Infinity.

Remember: A guru, a teacher, a messiah, a master is a technical know-how person. If it doesn't work for you, find another technique. If that doesn't work, find another technique. Every part doesn't fit every car.

The ultimate teacher is the Guru *within you.* That Guru is not a person. The Guru is Consciousness, like an ocean where you can totally immerse yourself and come out washed and clean. The Guru is the secret chamber of your inner Self. The Guru is that wisdom which you have attained and which you experience within when you overcome confusion, when the body and mind are on one side and your higher Self is on one side. The Guru is a vibration. The Guru can be awakened by a word of wisdom coming through a person who has attained a state of mental consciousness, a state of being that allows that person to direct or guide or speak the Infinite Truth under all circumstances.

## Creating through Vibration

We all have something in common. We all breathe, therefore we all vibrate. That vibration is the source of our life. Your total life is nothing without this activity. You are constantly vibrating, constantly interacting with the Universal vibration. The moment you don't vibrate, you are dead as a finite unit. Death is nothing but non-vibration of a finite unit. That's all death is. One who experiences the fact that life is a vibration, that life is a come and go, such a person is enlightened. That person is liberated.

It is not possible that you will *not* create anything, because you are a vibration. You are constantly creating as you vibrate, like it or not. Your vibration will create an action-reaction in relation to the Universal vibration. It does not matter who you are or what you have achieved, it only matters how you now radiate. The job of the human being is to radiate through the finite self the infinite Light.

You need to start understanding that you are the creative source and nucleus of the whole vibratory effect. The moment you understand that, your problem is solved. The moment you know that you are You, your problems are over. The moment you know that you are You, God and you are one, because you are the Creator and God is the Creator.

God vibrates, you vibrate, and the universe vibrates. If you want to get out of your karma, there is only one way, vibrate the Infinite as you breathe in and out. Whenever you vibrate that you are an Infinite-finite creation of the Infinite-finite Creator, then the Creator has to stand by you.

Those who learn to live on this primal vibration of God, they are the bright-faced, they are the light of Light, and their job is done. You can pinpoint such a person by the way you hear just one sentence. You can know how divine that person is. You will hear a Universal language coming from a Universal consciousness.

You too can be judged from the vibration you make–the language you speak and the way you relate to other people. Any word you speak exists. It is there as vibration. Word is a cause and an effect. You cannot escape from word. Realizing that you can't escape, word is your basic duty. If you remember that God sits on the top of your tongue, you will be very cautious about what you do with it.

**Lessons for Living**

Whether you believe me or not, there is a chance for every person to become a perfect saint. All training and all knowledge is meant for only one purpose, and the purpose is very simple and clear: that you may be in a position to control your mental self as well as you control your physical body. To be calm is the highest achievement of the self. When you react, you are known. When you don't react, you are Unknown. If you are trying to find the Unknown, all you have to do is not react. There is only one simple thing you have to practice: Do not react.

Be innocent. The highest prized quality is one's own innocence. No matter how clever and diplomatic and shrewd and intellectually creative you are, you are basically no-thing—because the beauty of the person lies in complete innocence. You have to transmigrate your existing being to a non-existing being. Learn to exist in the state of nonexistence; that is Reality. No-thing is everything and everything is no-thing. When you become no-thing, but tune into everything, then everything straightens out.

Levitate. Levitation is when you look at anything and you are not in it. You may hate, but you are not in the hatred. You may love, but you are not in the love. You may speak, but you are not in the speech. You may be silent, but you are not in the silence. You may act, but you do not have direction. When you surmount the consequences, you become *alive*. Bliss is a constant state of mind where one does not feel disturbed either by gain or by loss.

Relax. Don't run after God. God will run after you provided you know how to stay clear, provided you know love, provided you know how to stand honest. Self-relaxation is the highest discipline. If God knows you can relax, God will love you. There are many ways to feel relaxed. One is to feel that you are a part of the universe and that the universe is a part of you. You are just as beautiful as the universe. Without you, the universe is not beautiful, and you are not beautiful without the universe.

The physical body is a temple. Take care of it. The mind is energy. Regulate it. The Soul is God's projection. Represent It. All knowledge is false if the Soul is not projected, represented, and experienced with fidelity in the body and mind.

Live as *royal* saints. Nobody shall walk over you, but nobody who needs you shall be deprived of your strength. Be carefree, not careless. Carelessness is a deficiency, it happens because of laziness. You don't put forth effort. To be carefree is to use your higher Mind. You do your best. You feel good and keep up. Let the results be with God.

You are traveling all the time. Travel light, live light, spread the Light, be the Light.

# 2
# Paramahansa Yogananda

*Paramahansa Yogananda was born in India in 1893. He was a God-seeker from a very early age. While still a youth, he became a disciple of Swami Sri Yukteswar Giri, one of a line of exalted gurus. The story of his meeting and early life with the Swami is detailed in Yogananda's popular book, Autobiography of a Yogi. Beginning in the 1920's and continuing until his passing in 1952, Yogananda carried out his spiritual work in the United States through his Self-Realization Fellowship. His message reached millions, religious and non-religious alike. His image was featured on the cover of The Beatle's classic album, Sergeant Pepper's Lonely Heart Club Band. The materials presented here were extracted and gently edited from selections of his writing and lectures that appeared in Man's Eternal Quest (Los Angeles: Self-Realization Fellowship, 1975).*

## The Descent of Consciousness

Before creation existed, there was Cosmic Consciousness: Spirit, God, the Absolute... ever-existing, ever-conscious, ever-new Bliss beyond form and manifestation. When creation came into being, Cosmic Consciousness "descended" into the physical universe where it manifests as Universal Consciousness. Christians call this Christ Consciousness. The Hindu scriptures refer to it as Kutashtha Chaitanya. It is the omnipresent, pure reflection of God's Intelligence and Consciousness inherent–and yet hidden–within all creation.

When this omnipresent intelligence further "descends" into the physical body of a man or woman, it becomes Soul, or Super-consciousness: the ever-existing, ever-conscious, ever-new bliss of God individualized by encasement in the body. When the Soul becomes identified with that body, it "descends" further and manifests as ego, mortal consciousness.

Spirit: Cosmic Consciousness
∇∇∇∇
Christ: Universal Consciousness
∇∇∇
Soul: Super-consciousness
∇Δ∇
ego: mortal consciousness

The Soul is challenged to climb back up the ladder of consciousness into Spirit. We have come down from God, and we re-ascend to God, reuniting the Soul with the Spirit. We have seemingly become separated from God, and we must consciously reunite. We must rise above the delusion of separation and realize our oneness and sameness with God.

The poet Milton wrote of the soul of man and how it might regain paradise. Milton was right. This is our purpose and goal: to regain the lost paradise of Soul consciousness by which each one of us knows that she or he is, and ever has been, one with Spirit. God is the objective; consciousness of God's presence is what we should work toward. The Bhagavad Gita says: "He who absorbs himself in Me, with his Soul immersed in Me, him I regard, among all classes, as the most equilibrated."

As human beings we are very much privileged, for among all God's creatures we alone have the physical, mental, and spiritual endowment necessary to seek God, to find God, to know God, and to understand God's language of silence. Whether or not you believe in yourself as a Soul, you are nonetheless bound by the cosmic law to develop—consciously or unconsciously—your deeper nature. Respecting that law, you are compelled to learn how to use your mind so that you can evolve and realize your Oneness with the Creator.

Learn how to cultivate the consciousness of Spirit. That is why you were born a human being. You were created under the evolutionary law that you might exercise *your* Divine powers to find God.

## God-Realization

There are basically two approaches to God-realization: the outer way and the inner, or transcendental, way. The outer way is by right activity. You love and serve humankind... with your consciousness centered in God. Every good quality that you express in thought and action is meant to yield the hidden nectar of God's presence; and does so, if your inner perception is deep enough.

The inner, or transcendental, way is by esoteric meditation. Through meditation, you realize all the things you are not, and discover that which you are. You realize: "I am not the breath; I am not the body, neither bones nor flesh. I am not the mind or feeling... I am that which is *behind* the breath, body, mind, and feeling."

When you go behind and beyond the consciousness of this world, knowing that you are not the body or the mind, and yet aware as never before that you *exist*, you realize that you are simply That... That, in which is rooted everything in the universe! You are Divine consciousness.

To spend your time just playing with life and not finding God is wasting the divinely bestowed power within you. It is all right to enjoy life. However, the secret of happiness is: not to become attached to anything. Enjoy the smell of the flower, but see God in it. That is yoga, union with God.

It is not necessary to go to the forest or live in a cave to overcome attachments and find God. Wherever we may be, worldly habits will hold us fast until we free ourselves from them. The yogi learns to find God in the cave of the heart. Wherever he goes, he carries with him the blissful consciousness of God's presence. Anyone who has established God in the Soul temple is a yogi.

I suggest you wrest your mind from the mirage of the senses and habit. Why be deluded like that? I am pointing out to you a Land more beautiful than anything here can ever be. I am telling you of a Happiness that will intoxicate you night and day—you won't need sense temptations to enthrall you. Discipline your mind and your body. Control your senses. Banish the spiritual ignorance that makes you think this mortal life is *real*. Find God!

If only people knew wherein lies their own good! All great teachers declare that within this body is the immortal Soul, a spark of that which sustains all. One, who knows one's Soul, knows this truth: "I am beyond everything finite; I now see that the Spirit, alone in space with its ever-new joy, has expressed itself as the vast body of nature. I am the stars, I am the waves, I am the Life of all; I am the laughter within all hearts, I am the smile on the faces of flowers and in each Soul. I am the Wisdom and Power that sustain all creation." You must discover your own divinity and win the kingdom of God for yourself.

Befriend the Self within you and the Self will save you. It is the gravest insult to the Self to die believing you are a mortal being. Seize the God within you and realize that the Self is Divinity.

Find God! But don't seek God with any ulterior motive. Instead, cling to God's presence with devotion–unconditional, one-pointed, steady devotion. You must work, but let God work through you; this is the best part of devotion. If you are constantly thinking that God is walking through your feet, working through your hands, accomplishing through your will, you will know God.

When your love for God's presence is as great as your attachment to your mortal body, God will come to you and you to God. You will have found God. God-union is a joyous experience, a splendid Light in which you behold the countless worlds floating in a vast bed of joy and bliss.

If you are interested in finding God, and choose the outer way, then you must work, eat, walk, laugh, cry, meditate–only for God. In so doing, you will be truly happy: serving God, loving God, and communing with God. It is when you persistently, selflessly perform every action with love-inspired thoughts of God that God will come to you. Then you realize that you are the Ocean of Life, which has become the tiny wave of each life.

When in every action you think of God before you act, while you are performing the action, and after you have finished it, God will be revealed to you. You should also develop discrimination, so that you prefer spiritually constructive, God-conscious activity to work performed without any thought of God. That is the way of knowing God through activity.

But greater than activity, devotion, or reason, is meditation. That is the inner way to find God. I often say that this body is a switchboard and the five senses are its telephone instruments. Through them I am in touch with the world; but when I don't wish to communicate, I shut off my five senses and live in the inexpressible joy of God. God gave us reason that we might find freedom from the delusion of mortality. Realize that you are the Soul! Remember that the Feeling behind your feeling, the Will behind your will, the Power behind your power, the Wisdom behind your wisdom *is* the Infinite God.

Look within *yourself*. Remember, the Infinite is everywhere. Diving deep into Super-consciousness, you can speed your mind through Eternity. By the power of mind, you can go farther than the farthest star. The searchlight of mind is fully equipped to throw its super-conscious rays into the innermost heart of Truth. Use it to do so. Unite the heart's feeling and the mind's reason in a perfect balance. In the castle of calmness, again and again cast off identification with earthly titles and plunge into deep meditation to realize your divine royalty.

To be able to concentrate is essential for spiritual progress; without concentration, you shall never find God. Learn how to shut out of your consciousness all sounds and other earthly distractions. Unless you can cut off sounds from your consciousness, you cannot reach God.

So long as even a little tremor of thought and mental restlessness is present, you cannot reach cosmic consciousness. But as soon as your consciousness is right, God is there. God isn't hiding from you; you are hiding from God. The more peace you feel during concentration and the longer you concentrate, the deeper you will go in God. When in deep meditation you see any inner Light, try to hold it and feel you are inside it, one with it. That is where God is. Try to realize you are that Light of God.

However to meditate truly is to concentrate solely on Spirit. This is esoteric meditation. It is the highest form of activity that one can perform, and it is the most balanced way to find God. If you work all the time, you may become mechanical and lose God in preoccupation with your duties; and if you seek God only through discriminative thought, you may lose God in the labyrinths of endless reasoning; and if you cultivate only devotion for God, your development may become merely emotional. But esoteric meditation, opening fully to Spirit alone, combines and balances all these approaches.

The beauty of God is vast. To enjoy flowers for their loveliness is good; but far greater is to see behind their purity and beauty the face of God. To be carried away by music for its own sake cannot compare with hearing God's creative Voice in it. Though God is immanent in the finite beauties of creation, it is wisdom to realize one's eternal Self beyond form and finitude.

### Understanding God

God is beyond comprehension by mind and intellect. Powerful as they are, their scope is insufficient to contain God. The Originless Immeasurable is God. Omnipresent in the farthest reaches of space, God is in the distant stars...*and* in you and me. God is conscious every moment in every place.

God is not mind. God created mind and is beyond it. So the human mind is incapable of a true conception of God. However, though mind is incapable of encompassing Omnipresence, it is nevertheless able to *feel* God. If you use the mind properly, you can understand how God is beyond mind and intellect; and how God's true nature can be felt only through the Soul's power of intuition.

Where the Infinite becomes the finite, there is a point of contact: the Super-conscious mind. That mind can feel God. When we expand the ordinary mind until it impinges on the Super-conscious mind, we are able to feel God's presence. We must find God's consciousness through the intuitive Super-conscious mind, the nucleus of mind with divine Intelligence. If we attune our consciousness with God's consciousness, and remain in that current of bliss, we will feel *at-one* with God. Only in this state, attuned to God's consciousness within, can we hope to discover how God has condensed Consciousness into the multitudinous finite forms of creatures and the universes they inhabit.

In order to know God, you must become like God. As human beings, we have God-given power to cast away every habit and limitation and spread our consciousness throughout creation, penetrating not only the hearts of all creatures, but reaching out beyond the stars. Our native vastness encompasses even greater space. Such tremendous possibility lies within us!

We are Infinite! I live in that sphere of Infinity, and am conscious of the body only once in a while. You may be limited now; but when by deep, daily meditation you become able to transfer your consciousness from the finite to the Infinite, you will be free. You are not meant to be a prisoner of the body. You are a child of God; you must live up to that Divine birthright.

### The Visible and the Invisible

Space is divided into two parts or aspects. On one side of space is creation. On the other side is God alone; creation is completely absent. That is the world of the "dark-less dark" and the "light-less light." In this boundless stretch of Eternity behind creation, God alone lives in the unqualified Consciousness of ever-existing, ever-conscious, ever-new Bliss. No world or any other created thing exists in God's Consciousness in that part of Infinity where God reigns as the Absolute. But on the other side of space, God is aware of everything–all creation–*within* that Consciousness.

The same duality is true of human consciousness, for God has given you the opportunity to observe in your own consciousness the operation of the same laws that govern the universe. Your being has two sides–one visible, the other invisible. With open eyes you behold objective creation, and yourself in it. With closed eyes you see nothing, a dark void; yet your consciousness, even when dissociated from form, is still keenly aware and operative.

If in deep meditation you penetrate the darkness behind closed eyes, you behold the Light from which all creation emerges. Going still deeper, your experience transcends even this manifested Light and enters the All-Blissful Consciousness–beyond all form, yet infinitely more real, tangible, and joyous than any sensory or super-sensory perception.

I tell you that right behind you is God. Live no longer in ignorance of God's presence. Penetrate the darkness with your meditation. Don't stop until you find God. There is so much to know! So much to see within! In the quietness that you experience when your eyes are closed, don't feel you are alone. God is with you. Why should you think God is not? God is with you every minute of your existence, yet the only way to realize this is to meditate on that. And those of you who do meditate should go deeper! Don't fall asleep at night until you actually feel some expression of the presence of God within you. Peer into that darkness until you discover its wondrous secrets that await you just beyond.

If you put a sealed jar of water in a tank of water—that which is in the jar is separated from that which surrounds the jar. But if you remove the lid, the water in the jar and the water in the tank can mingle. Similarly, ordinary people shut out God because their consciousness is sealed in by the lid of ignorance. God is all around, but they don't feel God. And they cannot feel God, within or without, until they remove the lid of ignorance and merge their consciousness with God's Consciousness, to discover God within themselves.

If you sink in material desire, you will suffocate. If you sink in the ocean of God, you will live forevermore. When the lid is removed by right methods of meditation, one feels the peace of God inside and outside the body. As you increase the length and depth of your meditations, you will find more and more peace, and an ever-new joy. Whatever else you may try, it will not produce the divine Consciousness that comes from meditation.

### The Dream Nature of the World

Please do not take your earth experiences too seriously. If you wish to gather great wisdom, cultivate the consciousness that this world and everything in it is only a dream. Be prepared for every kind of experience that may come to you, realizing that all are but dreams. Difficulties come to us in order to awaken us to the realization that this life *is* a dream. This lesson we all have to learn. Take it as such.

Remember that whatever comes will simply be another scene in the dream movie of God, projected into your mind's playhouse. You can go to a movie and see a picture of war and suffering, and afterward say, "What a wonderful picture!" So may you take this life as a cosmic picture show, and exercise the same detachment.

The root-cause of sorrow is in viewing the passing show with emotional involvement...with attachment.

If you continually keep yourself down, thinking to yourself, "I haven't lived as I ought to have lived," you only make yourself miserable. Rather, do your best and move on; and no matter what difficulties come, ever affirm, "It is all a dream. It will soon pass." Then no trouble can be a great trial for you. No happenings of the earth can in any way torture you again.

Live in the consciousness of Spirit, in that oneness with God wherein you know that life is a dream. I can see the dream nature of life and death anytime I wish. Hence I attach little importance to this body nor do I fear death. It is very easy to do when you make the effort.

I am working for God alone. Earth has no illusions for me; I have seen through them all. You too should realize that you are visiting this earth only temporarily; you are here solely to learn necessary lessons and to help all who cross your path. You do not know why you have been cast in a particular role, so you must learn what God expects of you. You are here today, tomorrow you are gone: a mere shadow in a cosmic dream. But behind the unreality of these fleeting pictures is the immortal reality of Spirit.

Death is not the end; it is a freeing of the consciousness from the prison of the physical dream-body. That release brings a sense of great freedom. However, even knowing this, we should never anticipate death. Rather, we should prepare our consciousness by meditation and God-communion, so that when physical death comes, in its time, we are able to look upon it as a dream, nothing more.

Realize that the acting out of whatever part you are called upon to play does not affect your real Being. Once you are out of this body, you realize you are not dead; you are free of the dream. At the end of every earthly incarnation, you are the same—the immortal Soul—untouched by sickness, sorrow, or death.

You are playing different parts in his cosmic movie-house, and you may not foresee what part will be assigned to you tomorrow.

You should be prepared for anything. Such is the law of life. Why sorrow, then, over life's experiences? This show does have a purpose: that you learn how to play the various parts of the life movie without identifying your Self with these roles.

Your aim is to find true peace and happiness *within* yourself and *beyond* yourself. These outer experiences should be only fun. Whether you are suffering in this life, or smiling with opulence and power, your consciousness should remain unchanged. If you can accomplish even-mindedness, nothing can ever hurt you.

The lives of all great masters show that they have achieved this blessed state. As written in the Bhagavad Gita, "The man who is calm and even-minded during pain and pleasure, the one whom these cannot ruffle, he alone is fit to attain Everlastingness." When you are awake in God, God will show you that you are unchanged, even though you have played countless parts in God's earth drama. Egotistical pride must go. It is a blind that prevents your seeing God as the sole Doer, the Director of the Cosmic Drama.

If you take every happening as you would if you were seeing someone else playing it in a motion picture, you will not grieve. Play your 365 roles each year with an inward smile and with the remembrance that you are only dreaming. Then you will never again be hurt by life.

God put you in this sensate physical form with the intention that you live in the world as an introspecting soul, enjoying the movies of creation without becoming identified with them. That is how God wants you to live: to demonstrate mind control not only when everything is rosy, but in the midst of your troubles also. When you manifest changelessness, you become royalty among souls. Changeless within, even though body and mind are constantly changing, you become one with changeless Infinity.

Learning to disconnect oneself mentally from the disturbance of sensations brings peace of mind. The person who remains untouched by the sensations that come and go, being neutral to their ever-changing stimuli, manifests the Soul's essential changelessness. To be free of sensations, one has to separate oneself mentally from the body. Therefore the saints teach mental detachment from both pleasure and pain.

To understand and experience "mental above-ness," one must practice it. A mind made strong by the practice of powerful and positive thinking is less affected by sensations of pleasure and pain. It recognizes sensations in the way God intended—as a form of academic experience.

Life here on earth appears futile and chaotic until you are anchored in the Divine. My greatest joy is to remind others of the importance and necessity of remembering God. It is because of "maya," the net of cosmic delusion which is thrown over us, that we entangle ourselves in mundane interests and forget God.

The only experience that is real, the only experience that brings happiness, is awareness of the presence of God. The greatest romance is with the Infinite. When you suddenly find God everywhere, when God comes and talks to you and guides you, the romance of divine love has begun.

You fail on the stage of life because you are trying to act a part differently from the one divinely designed for you. Accept the part you are playing, be it that of buffoon or king. Sometimes the buffoon attracts more attention than the king; so no matter how obscure your role, play it conscientiously. Realize that an aspect of the Infinite power of Spirit is performing through you on the stage of the world.

Tune yourself with that Spirit as it plays through you, and in this earth-drama you will play your part incredibly well. Never mind which part you have to play, always strive to act it well, in harmony with the direction of the Stage Manager, so that your little role can and will enlighten others. Human relationships are given to you to be idealized. You do this by doing little things... in an extraordinary way. Show others that God's creative principle works in you. But most of all, *you* be entertained by the Divine messages coming from your own Soul.

# 3
# Ramana Maharshi

*Ramana Maharshi (1879-1950) was considered one of the great spiritual teachers of modern-day India. He achieved Self-realization at the tender age of 17 and thereafter remained conscious of his identity with the Absolute. He followed no particular traditional system of teaching, but spoke always from his own experience of non-duality. His method of instruction was to direct visitors again and again to the true Self and to recommend, as a path to realization, a tireless form of self-inquiry featuring the question, "Who am I?" The materials presented here were abstracted and gently edited from The Spiritual Teaching of Ramana Maharshi (Shambala, 1988).*

## Practice Only for Ripe Souls

Self-realization is the realization of your own *true* nature. For you to be successful as a seeker of liberation, you must realize—without doubts or misconceptions—your *true* nature. This means that you must distinguish the Eternal from the transient and not swerve from your Eternal state. There is nothing other than or superior to this natural, Eternal state to be attained. In this state, you know yourself as "Self."

All mundane activities which are ordinarily called "effort" are performed with the aid of only a portion of the mind and with frequent breaks. But the act of Self-communion is intense activity which is performed with the *entire* mind and without break.

The partial mind thinks; it is restless and agitated. The *entire* mind is a tranquil State in which thoughts simply come to an end. This is the State of Self. If the moments that are wasted in thinking are instead spent on mindful *inquiry* into Self, Self-realization will be attained in a very short time.

The excellence of this practice lies in not giving room for even a single mental concept. This is known as the "practice of *knowledge*." It leads quickly to Self-realization, more quickly than other practices. However, the practice is suitable only for ripe souls. The rest cannot yet accept this straightforward approach and hence must follow different, more circuitous methods according to the state of their minds.

Self is your natural state. It is the mind that obstructs realization of your natural state. What is called "mind" is a wondrous—but Self-denying–power—that paradoxically resides within the Self. It causes all thoughts to arise. It causes the Self to momentarily forget itself. When you investigate what the mind is—through full-minded observation—the mind will disappear. Self will then shine through.

When the mind comes out of the Self, it comes out thinking... and creates first "you" and then "your world." Whenever the world is being experienced by you as real, it is your mind at work and the Self is forgotten. Being aware of your thoughts, you surmise the existence of something from which it starts and term that "your mind." However, when you probe deeply to see what it is, you find there is really no such "thing" as mind—neither yours nor anyone else's. When the mind has thus vanished, you again encounter the Eternal Self.

What exists in truth is the Self *alone*. The Self ***is*** the world; the Self ***is*** "I"; the Self ***is*** God. When the Self shines, the world does not appear. As the Self dims itself, the mind appears. Hence, realization of the Self will not be gained unless mind stops, thoughts stop, and the belief that the world is "real" is removed. The Self returns when there is absolutely no "I" thought, no "world" thought, even no thoughts about God. In that Silence, all is Self. All is God.

The world should be considered like a dream. Stop seeking what is other than the Self. Just as one who wants to throw away garbage has no need to analyze it and see what it is, so one who wants to know the Self has to reject all the inquiries and analysis that hide the Self. Not losing the Self through the mind is wisdom.

## The "I"-Thought

Of all thoughts that arise in the mind, the "I"-thought is the first. It is only after the rise of the "I"-thought that other thoughts arise in the mind. It is after the appearance of the first-person pronoun ("I") that the second and third person-pronouns ("you" and "it") appear; without the first-person pronoun there will not be the second and the third.

The "I"-thought is ego at work; it gives birth to the illusion of a separate self, a separate "I." Then when other thoughts arise from the "I" thought, these simply build on the original illusion, piling illusion on illusion—separating self from others and others from still others. The "I" treats this pile of thought-up illusions as the "real world" and believes it to be so. In turn, it treats the Self as "illusion."

When thoughts about the world arise, you should not pursue them. Instead inquire about where they came from and to whom they came. The answer that must emerge is that they came to me from "me." Thereupon, if one inquires about the source of this "me" with *full* mindedness (asking "Who am I?"), the mind will find its way back to its source. With repeated practice in this manner, the mind will master the skill of staying at its source, the Self. Therefore, to quiet the mind, you have only to *inquire* continually within yourself, "Who am I?" No answers, just the question.

The feeling that "I am doing this or that" is the hindrance. Ask yourself, "*Who* is doing this or that?" Remember who you *truly* are. Then what you are doing will not bind you in illusion. Let the mind run on automatically, as it will in any case. Make no effort either to do something about it or to renounce it. Your effort to do either is the bondage.

If you are destined to do something, you will do it; if not, you won't. Leave these things to the higher Power, to the Self. You are not apart from the Self. The Self is universal; so all actions will go on whether you strain yourself to be engaged in them or not. The show will go on of itself. However, if the Self is realized, there will be no mind that pretends to control the show. The Self will simply shine forth and the mind will not dominate.

The fact is you are ignorant of your blissful State. Your mind-produced ignorance draws a veil over pure Self (which is Bliss). Inquiry into "Who am I?" aims only to remove this veil of ignorance, this wrong knowledge, this false identification with the body, mind, world, etc. This false identification must go, and then the Self alone will remain. Your duty is to ***be***, and not to be "this" or "that."

The whole Truth can be summed up as: "I am that I am." The whole method for Self-realization can be summarized as: "Be *still*." And what does *stillness* mean? It means "Destroy your false self!" Every name and form is a falsehood and the cause of trouble. "I-I" is Self. "I am this" is the ego. When the "I" is purely I, it is the Self. When it flies off at a tangent and says "I am this or that, I am such and such!" it is ego.

Whatever form your inquiry may take, you must finally come to the one-and-only-one-I, which is the Self. All the distinctions made between "you" and "others" are merely signs of ignorance. The "I-Supreme" alone is. To think otherwise is to delude. When you withdraw from the superficialities of a personal "I" in a physical world, drop all thoughts and mindfully seek the source of thought, where then is the "world" and where then is the "I?"

**The "I-Am-the-Body" Idea**

What is the significance of the Crucifixion? The body is the cross. Jesus, the son of man, is the ego or "I-am-the-body" idea. When the son of man is crucified on the cross, the ego perishes, and what survives is the Absolute Being. It is the resurrection of the Glorious Self, of the Christ—the Son of God. What appears to be a death is actually a Birth. The Eternal, blissful, natural state is smothered by a life identified with the body. In ending that identification, the Eternal, positive existence is revealed.

The illusory physical world, which you say is real, is mocking you for seeking to prove its reality while of your own reality you remain ignorant. That alone is real which exists by itself, which reveals itself by itself, and which is Eternal and unchanging. So what is the nature of the physical world? It is perpetual change, a continuous, interminable flux without Self-consciousness... arising, like the mind, from the Self and destined to merge back within the Self. If you take the physical appearance to be "reality," you will never know Reality itself. Until you give up the idea that the world is "reality," your mind will continue to chase after itself and perpetuate the illusions of "the world" and of "you."

The body is itself a mere projection of the mind; and the mind is but a poor reflection of the radiant Heart that *resides* in the Self. This spiritual Heart is not an organ of the body. All that you can say of the Heart is that it is the very core of your being: that with which you are really identical, whether you are awake, asleep, or dreaming, whether you are engaged in work or immersed in meditation. But people do not understand this. They cannot help thinking in terms of the physical body and the physical world.

The physical body cannot subsist apart from pure Consciousness of the Self. Body consciousness is merely a miniature reflection of pure Consciousness. It is only a reflected ray, as it were, of the Self. Pure Self-Consciousness—wholly free of the physical body and transcending the mind—is a matter of direct experience. Sages recognize this, you do not.

Sages know their bodiless, eternal existence just as the layperson knows his or her bodily existence. And, for these sages, the experience of Consciousness can be with bodily awareness as well as without it. In the bodiless experience, the sage is beyond time and space in the radiant Heart.

The supreme state of Self-awareness is never absent; it transcends the three states of mind (asleep, dreaming, and awake) as well as life and death. The death of the physical body is not the extinction of the Self. Its relation to the body is not limited by birth and death, and its place in the physical body is not circumscribed by one's experience felt at a particular place, as for instance between the eyebrows or at the crown of the head.

### To See God is to *Be* God

Realization is nothing to be gained afresh. It is already there. All that is necessary is to get rid of the thought "I have not realized." There is no reaching the Self. If the Self were to be reached, it would mean that the Self is not *here and now* but is yet to be obtained. Then, should it be reached, it could also be lost. So it would not be permanent and eternal. And what is not permanent and eternal is not worth striving for. So I say the Self is not reached. You *are* the Self; you are already that.

As the Self is all-pervasive, its natural state is one free of limiting concepts. This also means that the limiting sense of "I" and "mine" exists no longer. So long as there is the idea that "I" am the Self, there cannot be a realization of truth. The beauty lies in remaining free from all delusion. Paradoxically, getting rid of attachment to one's self is equivalent to abiding more in the Self. This involves removing all the attachments which have crept into the mind through thought.

The ego will ultimately submit only when it recognizes and is absorbed within the higher Power. To see God is to *be* God. God alone is. To abide in the Self, you must love the Self, love God. Surrender can take effect only when done with full knowledge as to what real surrender means.

You cannot bargain with God or demand favors at God's hands. Until the tendency to identify with objects of desire or states of awareness is destroyed, the ego cannot become pure and merge within its Source. The false identification of oneself with the body or with the "I-am-the-body" idea must go before good results can follow.

Unhappiness is due to the mind and the ego-ness it projects; with it comes all your trouble. When you deny the "I"-thought and scorch it by ignoring it, you are free. If you accept it, it will impose limitations on you and throw you into a vain struggle to transcend these limitations. Don't you see the tangled knot that the "I"-thought produces?

Whether you continue in the household or go to the forest for meditation, your mind will continue to haunt you. It will make you think that you really are a householder or a monk in the forest. Hence, it is no help to find your true self by changing the environment. The mental obstacles move with you. They do not disappear when you substitute one environment for another. They may even increase greatly in the new surroundings.

Instead of renouncing one's physical family and heading off for a cave, it is better to stay where one is and renounce one's mental family of fancies and doubts. This is the real asceticism.

## Self-Inquiry

The starting point for deep inquiry is recognition that the "I" must be understood. To whichever school of thought you may belong, you should first find out what the "I" is. Then it will be time enough to discover what comes next, whether the "I" will get merged in the Supreme Being or stand apart. Let us not forestall the conclusion, but keep an open mind. Instead of indulging in mere speculation, devote yourself here and now to the search for the truth that is ever within you.

Self-inquiry is the one infallible means, the only direct one, to realize the unconditioned, absolute Being that you really are. The very purpose of Self-inquiry is to focus the entire mind at its Source. It is not a case of one "I" striving to be a better "I." Much less is Self-inquiry an empty formula, for it involves an intense activity of the *entire* mind to keep steadily poised in pure Self-awareness. Self-inquiry alone can reveal the truth that neither the ego nor the mind have independent existence. It enables one to realize pure, undifferentiated Self-being, the Absolute.

Happiness is inherent to the Self. On those occasions which you consider pleasurable, you are diving into the Self. That diving results in Self-existent bliss. The association of ideas is responsible for the false notion that you have to look outside of yourself to find bliss; while, in fact, bliss is inseparable you're your true nature. When your diving is done consciously, with the conviction that you are identical with the happiness and bliss that is verily the Self, the one Reality, you are truly Self-realized.

You are really the Infinite, pure Being, the Self Absolute. You are always that Self and nothing but that Self. Therefore, you can never be really completely ignorant of the Self; your ignorance is a veil to be removed. Know that true Self-knowledge does not create a new and somehow better being for you; it only removes your "ignorant ignorance." Ego-consciousness is a contradiction in terms. It is no existence, no consciousness, at all.

# 4
# J. Krishnamurti

*Jiddu Krishnamurti (1895-1986) was a world-renowned educator, lecturer, and spiritual guide. In his early years, he was associated with the Theosophical Society and thought by them to be the "teacher of the age." He soon denounced this idea as well as several others of the Society and went off on his own. He traveled extensively giving hundreds of talks each year, often to audiences of a thousand or more. He wrote several books and nearly a hundred others were compiled from his talks and discussions. The materials included here were extracted and gently edited from The Urgency of Change (London: V. Gollancz, 1971) and Reflections on the Self (Chicago: Open Court, 1977).*

## Fragmented Understanding

It is very important to understand something right from the beginning. If you don't understand this, you will simply get more and more confused. Listen closely: Your response to any thing or any person blocks seeing what is as it truly is. When there is a psychological response to any thing or person, this response is always a conditioned response. It is a response triggered by past memory, past experiences. Thus, it is something that you concoct and not that thing or person as it is that moment. When you identify with the response, you do not *see* with *total* perception... your seeing and understanding are fragmented and exaggerated.

In responding, you give birth to what we shall call the "me" that stands apart from and relates through memory to that thing or person, to that "not-me." The "me" is also a creation of memory. It, too, is a conditioned response, a fragmented and exaggerated "someone" that you create from past memory and experience and take to be the one and the same "me." When you identify with the "me," you do not *know* yourself with *total* perception... your understanding of yourself is fragmented and exaggerated. This also must be understood.

There is the physical space that separates you from people and things, and there is the psychological space between you and them. We are not talking about the physical space. We are talking about the psychological space.

It is only when you begin to feel psychological space, not explain or analyze it, that it begins to dissolve. This space has come into being because of thought. Thought creates psychological distance between you and other people and things, between ideas and reality... and then thought struggles to close the distance it has created. This is the game and it is always unsuccessful.

This is not just something you alone are doing. Everyone is doing it to themselves and each other. They are inventing psychology distances and then inventing ways to close them. It is all happening in the mind and played out through fragments of understanding. There is no space-ful awareness, no total *seeing* of what is really there.

Fragmented understanding, where there is a "me" and a "not-me," is most dangerous and destructive. And fragmented understanding is exactly what we encounter everywhere. The respected world leader, the revered religious leader, the successful businessman, the high-powered technician—even the visionary artist—all of them see only partially. They are inattentive to the *moment* and, instead, they re-construct things and themselves from past prejudices and biases.

As they play a great part in the world, their partial and distorted perceptions become the accepted norms and their fragmented understanding becomes the general understanding. This makes them very destructive people. Even if their intentions are noble, their perceptions are not.

All conflict is rooted in this psychological division. When there is no such division of "me" and "not-me," when there is instead *total* perception, you immediately stop producing conflict. In short, where there is "me," there is a producer of conflict; where there is a mind empty of "me," there is freedom from conflict production.

The empty mind is simply aware and intelligent. The whole of life is met in every moment. Each moment is its own unique challenge met conflict-free. To meet this challenge inadequately, with fragmentary perception and divisive understanding, is a crisis in living.

All human existence is in relationship to the world, to others, and to our own being. Changing the world radically must mean changing the nature of these relationships. And this radical revolution, if it is to be a true revolution, must be *immediate*... it cannot take time. If time is involved, then here comes the past and here comes the "me." With the "me" present, there is no real change, just a continuation of what has been. Just more conflict production, perhaps in new forms.

All attempts to change ourselves or our world lead only to more disorder. They create psychological distances between "what is" and "what ought to be." And psychological distances, as we have just explored, are conflict-producers. We have to stop creating more conflict, we have to stop interfering with the world, imposing our fragmented being and exaggerated understanding upon it. We have to stop doing anything about it that creates psychological distances.

Be simple. This is the miracle of perception: to perceive with a heart and mind that are completely cleansed of the desire to change things. Such *negation* is the most positive action. Your very being—totally present and awakened—becomes the force for radical change.

**Your Problem is the Mind**

The way you perceive is what *you are*. The way you perceive determines the very quality of your being. Righteousness, in contrast to destructive behavior, is in purely *looking*—which is full attention without the intervention of measure and idea. To simply *look*, without distortion, is Love. It is the highest human virtue.

Thinking and feeling are one. Your problem is not the integration of the different fragments of your being, but the understanding of the mind and heart which are one and the same. Your problem is not how to get rid of social classes or how to build better utopias or breed better politicians or new religious leaders. Your problem is the mind. Of course, it is not just you that needs to recognize the true problem. It is a crisis for humankind.

To come to this understanding, this realization, not theoretically but to *see* it actually, is the highest form of Intelligence. Then you are your own guru and you are your own disciple: you understand yourself *totally*. This understanding cannot be learned from another.

Nobody can free the mind of the "me" for you—no guru, no drug, no mantra. It is not something to be chased after because that too is a response. All that you have to do is non-respond: be *aware* from the beginning to the end and not become inattentive in the middle of it. With full attention, there is no room for a response and no room for penetration by the "me." In *seeing* without psychological distance, there is a mind empty of the "me." This mind has a different quality, a different kind of awareness.

When one is conforming to a pattern—a tradition, a conclusion, an ideal, an assumption, and so on—there is always a contradiction present between what one actually *is* and that pattern. There is always this conflict. With pattern-less, non-conditioned *seeing*, there is awareness of the world without any contradiction, conflict, or judgment. By suspending judgment, you instantly eradicate the principle of psychological division, the principle of "me" standing apart from "not-me." *Seeing* is without any judgment. In the *seeing*, there is no "me." There is either the "me" or the *seeing*, there cannot be both. The "me" cannot *see*, cannot be aware.

All forms of analysis, judgment, descriptions, and even most spiritual practices have duration, they are not instantaneous. Hence they are conflict producers, even when approached with good intentions. Total *seeing*, total *hearing*, and total *awareness* happen instantaneously or not at all. Time duration to get from here to there cannot enter into this. Total perception can only be out of silence, not out of a chattering, searching, or achieving-oriented mind. It is only a quiet mind that *sees* totally.

The question, "How to get a quiet mind?" does not arise. There is the simple truth that the mind must be quiet if there is to be *seeing*. Finally realizing this truth frees the mind from chattering. Total perception, which is intelligence, is then operating, and not some ethical prescription that says, "You must be silent in order to *see.*" *Seeing* is total attention right now. Practice of any sort is total inattention. Never practice; you can only practice mistakes.

Total *awareness* is an observation, both outer and inner, in which direction has stopped. You are aware, but the thing or person or situation of which you are aware is not being encouraged nor nourished. Awareness is not concentration on a thing. It is not an action of the will choosing what it will be aware of, and then analyzing it to bring about a certain result. If you focus your concentration away from the total toward something or someone—that is, put all your thought energy in that direction—then this thing or person is instantly distorted and exaggerated. This prevents total *awareness* and conflict-free action.

Problems persist because you fail to look at them with choice-less awareness and unobstructed intelligence. You continue to look partially and prejudicially and thereby allow them to continue and fester. So the task is to *see* the problems so completely so that, in that very seeing, you have understood the root not only of this problem but of every problem. You realize that every problem is rooted in not-seeing and in the conflict that arises immediately out of your mind when you do not *see* totally.

Perceiving, seeing, and understanding are instantaneous: you understand instantly or not at all. If your consciousness is changed radically, profoundly—no, revolutionized rather than changed—then you are poised to affect the consciousness of the whole of mankind.

Please see the truth of this. Knowing this, you become tremendously responsible. You are not just worrying a little bit about your own particular little worry. You have the ability to change the world if you do not retreat from this *total* awareness.

### Emptying Oneself

As I have indicated, true quiet—free of the chattering mind—comes with the loss of the "me." The "me" is an echo from your past; it has nothing to do with what is *now*. When there is thought, there is the "me" speaking. It is the past living as the present, so there is no living in the Present at all. All continuity is thought, to be sure; but when there is continuity, there is nothing really new. Either you live in the past and never experience the Present, or you live totally different—that is the whole point.

The craving for certainty, for security, is one of the major activities of the brain, and it is this compelling urge that has to be watched—and not merely twisted or forced in another direction or made to conform to some preset pattern. True, the brain must respond when it sees danger... this is intelligent. Its actions are also necessary when dealing with facts, such as how to get to the dentist's office. When I go to do something, thought has its place. But it has no place psychologically. It is not intelligent for the brain to breed psychological conflict.

It must be conditioned to recognize the danger of such division and fragmentation, much as it is conditioned to recognize the danger of certain physical events. To perceive the psychological danger, the brain has to be very alert and awake, much more so than it is when it deals with facts and things. The brain can deal with facts, things, and physical dangers through the automatic activation of memories. However, to overcome psychological conflict, it must be completely *awake* and spontaneous.

When the brain is completely awake in the Present, there is no fragmentation, no separation, no duality of "me" and "not-me." Seeing is no longer based upon conditioning and propaganda. The mind that is *awake* is quiet. This quietness from the "me" is the highest form of intelligence; it is neither personal nor impersonal, it is whole and immaculate. It defies description, because it has no attributes.

This is awareness, this is Love, and this is the highest. When the artist is playing beautifully, there is no "me." There is love and beauty... and this is art. This is skill in action. And the greatest and most skillful art: living *totally* in the whole field of life. The sanity of the mind can only come when there is such quietness and wholeness.

Freedom is not an abstraction. It is the state of mind in which there is no form of resistance whatsoever. It is not like a river that accommodates itself to boulders here and there, going around or over them. In this freedom, there are no boulders at all... only the movement of the water. You must first understand what freedom is, then you will understand your boulders. It is not that you must first understand yourself, and then act. In the understanding, there is action without premeditation... it is activity itself, it is creation.

It is only when there is emptiness in oneself, an emptiness that comes with the total negation of everything one has been and should be and will be, that there is creation. It is only in this freedom from the "me" that something new can take place. The brain is conditioned to fear this emptiness and to produce thoughts that compare this emptiness with physical nothingness. True emptiness occurs when the fear and the thoughts are also negated. In this psychological "death" comes *understanding* and *perception*. Everything that exists has its very being in this freedom. Life is lived everywhere and nowhere, there are no frontiers.

### Beyond the Self

When there is the ending of the self, what takes place? Not at the end of life, not when the brain becomes deteriorated, but when the brain is very, very active, quiet, alive... what then takes place, when "me" is not?

We cannot find what is beyond the mind if we do not know, if we are incapable of facing, *what is*. And to face *what is* requires enormous attention, great passive awareness, observation without justification and without judgment... just to observe, just to listen. In that, there is transformation. In that, there is Happiness which is not measured by time, by the mind. There is a constant perception of Beauty without the accumulation of memories, there is the possibility of Joy everlasting.

Joy is not pleasure. You can't think and understand what Joy is. You can think about it and reduce it to pleasure, but the thing that is Joy, ecstasy, is not the product of thought. Pleasure is the movement of thought and thought can in no way cultivate Joy. You can invite pleasure, you can think about it, sustain it, nourish it, seek it out, pursue it, and hold it. But you cannot with Joy, with ecstasy. Joy happens naturally, easily, or not at all. If you pursue what has been joyous, then it is only a remembrance, a dead thing that you pursue.

Joy or Beauty or Happiness is never time-binding; these qualities are totally free of time... and so of culture. They are there when the self is not. The self is put together by time, by the movement of thought, by the known. In the abandonment of "me," in that *total* attention, that essence of Joy, Beauty, and Happiness is there. The letting go of "me" is not the calculated action of desire or will. Will is directive and so resistant, divisive, and conflict-breeding. The dissolution of the self is synonymous with total inward non-action and also synonymous with the presence of Beauty, Happiness, and Joy.

When you look at a cloud, at the light in that cloud, there is Beauty. Beauty is passion. To see the *beauty* of a cloud or the *beauty* of the light on a tree, there must be passion, there must be intensity. In this intensity, this passion, there is no sentiment whatsoever, no feeling of like or dislike. Ecstasy is not personal; ecstasy is not yours or mine, just as Love is not yours or mine.

Society and religion teaches us that if we can transcend ourselves, deny ourselves, put ourselves out of the way by dedicating our lives to something much greater and more vital than ourselves, we shall perhaps experience a bliss, a happiness which is not merely a physical sensation. Or, we are urged to stop thinking about ourselves through the cultivation of virtue, through discipline, through control, through dedicated practice.

But the person who is conscious of sacrificing her or his self, or the virtuous person who is conscious of pursuing virtue, can never find what is *real*. They may be very decent or spiritually-minded persons. But that is very different from those who understand Truth. For them, "truth" has not been pursued and found; it has simply come into being. Virtuous people aim to strengthen and ultimately perfect their virtuous selves; the person knowing Truth has no self to perfect. That person, knowing Truth, is self-less.

On those moments when the self, the "me," with all its memories and travails, with all its anxieties and fears, has completely ceased, one is then a being without any motive. One is then a being without the seed of self with its anxiety, ambition, frustration, its fear of not being, and the immense urge to be secure. And in that state, one is *aware* of an astonishing sense of immeasurable distance, of limitless space and being.

The whole movement of "my" thinking and all "my" activity is essentially based on the continuance of "myself" in one form or another. If I once *see* that, if I realize it, feel it with my whole being, then religion has quite a different meaning. Then spirituality is no longer a process of identifying myself with God, but rather the coming to being of a state in which there is only that *reality* and not the "me."

To gain this Self-knowledge, you must go very deeply into yourself without assuming anything, so that the mind has no deceptions, no illusions, so that it does not trick itself into visions and false states. Then, it is possible for the enclosing process of the self to come to an end—but not through any form of compulsion or discipline, because the more you discipline the self, the stronger the "me" becomes.

What is important is to go into all this very deeply and patiently, without taking anything for granted, so that one begins to find the ways, the purposes, the motives and directions of the mind. Then, I think, the mind comes to a state in which there is no identification at all, and therefore no effort to be something. Then, there is the cessation of the self and that is what is *real*.

Then the mind will discover that there is in fact unlimited space without a center. When once that has been found, there is freedom, there is order, and then Goodness and Beauty flower in the human mind.

# 5
# Bhagwan Shree Rajneesh

*Bhagwan Shree Rajneesh, later called simply Osho, was born in India in 1931. He was a highly popular and controversial spiritual leader who attracted over 200,000 devotees, many from Europe and the United States. He was a prolific writer with close to 500 book titles to his credit covering a wide range of esoteric and spiritual topics. His tombstone reads, "Never Born. Never Died. Only Visited the Planet Earth Between December 11, 1931 and January 19, 1990." The materials included here were extracted and gently edited from his book, My Way: The Way of the White Clouds (New York: Grove Press, 1975).*

## The Way of the White Clouds

I call my way, the way of the white clouds. The white cloud is not being used as a fact. It is used as a symbol, as a poetic symbol; as an indication of the possibility for a deep merger into the mysterious and the miraculous. A white cloud is a most mysterious thing, suddenly appearing, suddenly disappearing. No name, no fixed form. It is changing, it is becoming. It is formless, or continuously being formed—it is a flux.

A white cloud exists without any roots. It is an un-rooted phenomenon, grounded nowhere... or grounded in the nowhere. But still it exists. A white cloud really has no way of its own. It drifts. It has nowhere to reach, no destination, no destiny to be fulfilled, no end. You cannot frustrate a white cloud, because *wherever* it reaches is the goal. All dimensions belong to it, all directions belong to it. Nothing is rejected. Everything is, exists, in a total acceptability.

A white cloud hovers in the sky, timeless because there is no future and no mind to it. It is here and now. Every moment for it is total eternity. White cloud's way means a pathless path, a way-less way. Moving, but never leaving the moment. The goal remains here and now. Only a mind that is as purposeless as a white cloud truly can be called a "religious" mind. But that quality of mind is no more a "mind" at all. No mind, just presence... just being *here*. No resistance, no fight, nothing to be achieved, nothing to be lost.

Just enjoying the very existence, celebrating the moment, the joy, and the ecstasy of it. Just meditating on drifting, continuously contemplating the whole scene, and by and by being merged. I say drifting, not moving, not moving to a point—just drifting where so ever the winds lead that mind. The goal for the religious mind is realized every moment.

In stark contrast, there is the way of the restless, ego-driven mind. Now there *is* always a goal, a specific destination, that is somewhere else than right here. The mind starts thinking about that goal and how to reach it, it starts a process... and it likes this. It can flow, have its course, and have space to move. With purpose comes future, with future comes time. Now that mind is in *its* element. A restless mind is a seeking mind, a problem-solving mind, a mind needing to know.

### Society Cannot Allow Ecstasy

Society has done a great disservice. The education, the culture, and the culturing agencies, parents, teachers—they have done a great disservice. They have made miserable creatures out of ecstatic creatures. Every child is born ecstatic. Every child is born a god or goddess. And everyone dies just a miserable mad person.

In our society, misery seems to be downhill—easy to slip down into; ecstasy, in contrast, seems to be uphill—a real struggle for us to reach. But, free of society, the reverse is true. Ecstasy is downhill, ecstasy is natural. Misery is very difficult to achieve... but you and others with the help of society have achieved it, you have done the anti-natural. Nobody wants to be miserable and still everybody is miserable.

To be separate as an ego is the base of all misery. To be one, to be flowing, with whatsoever life brings to you, to be in it so intensely, so totally, that you are no more, you are lost... then everything is blissful. Unless you recover, unless you reclaim your childhood, you will not be able to become like the white clouds I have been talking about. This is the whole work for you, the whole practice: how to regain childhood, how to reclaim it. If you can become childlike again then there is no misery.

The old crust that society has created around you, the imprisonment in misery, can be broken. You can come out of it, even for a few moments, and be ecstatic.

A word of caution, however. If you fully recover from misery, most everyone will think you are mad. Whenever you spontaneously and constantly feel ecstatic and blissful, people become both suspicious and jealous. With "good" intentions, society will try in every way to put you back into the old state of misery. Psychoanalysts will help, psychiatrists will help, to bring you to the normal misery.

Society cannot allow ecstasy, it goes against the grain. If people become ecstatic, the whole society will have to change. Politics will have to change. Religion will have to change. Social mores will have to change. Lots of people will feel left out, cheated, and uncomfortable. So we are talking about real revolution. And I challenge you to be a revolutionary... to regain your birthright.

So what to do? You live a life as if you are *not*, you travel the way-less way. You become a white cloud. The less you are, the more healthy you will be. The less you are, the more weightless you will be. The less you are, the more you will be divine and blissful. So, dissolve yourself before that mystery, annihilate yourself before that mystery, and disperse yourself before that mystery. You be no more, and let the mystery be so total that you are absorbed in it. Suddenly, a new door opens, a new perception is achieved. Everything loses its boundary; divisions melt away, everything is one. Become a cloud with no form, with no name. And then drifting starts.

The fear is that you will be out of control. But I suggest a new control. Not the control of a manipulating mind, but the control of a witnessing Self. And I tell you: that control is the supreme control possible; and that control is so natural that you never feel you are controlling. The control happens spontaneously with witnessing. Whatever you do, you must encounter and consciously witness the whole process. You must see it whole, but also see through and beyond it... not become lost within it. That's all.

## Create the Effect

You are certainly aware of one of the most basic scientific laws, that cause and effect is the innermost link of all processes of life. You create the cause and the effect follows. You put the seed in the soil and it will sprout. If the cause is there, then the tree will follow. The fire is there—you put your hand in it and it will burn. You take poison and you will die. You arrange for the cause and then the effect follows. Society sets up the conditions where ego is nurtured and misery follows.

Religion knows about a *second* law which is deeper than the first. Religion says: Produce the effect and the cause follows. This is absolutely absurd in scientific terms. Science says: If the cause is there, the effect follows. Religion says the converse is also true. You create the effect, and see... the cause follows. Jesus said: "Seek ye the Kingdom of God, then all else will follow." He understood the second law.

And I tell you it is easier to start with the effect because the effect depends totally upon you; the cause may not be so dependent on you. Cause is perhaps beyond you, outside your reach. Effect is always within you. Choose happiness and then see what happens. Or, choose ecstasy and see what happens. You will witness your whole life changing immediately and you will see miracles happening around you—because now you have created the effect and causes will have to follow.

This will look magical; you can even call it "the law of magic." The first is the law of science and the second is the law of magic. Religion is magic and you can be the magician.

There is an old saying: Weep and you weep alone; laugh and the whole world laughs with you. If you can create the effect and be ecstatic, even the trees, the rocks, the sand, and the clouds will dance with you. Then, the whole existence becomes a dance, a celebration. But it depends on you. You must create the effect. It looks very difficult because you have been taught differently and have not tried it yet. Give it a try!

Life energy has its own ways of working. When you act totally, it becomes the real. The only thing is, for it to work, the egocentric actor must not be there. Dissolve the actor into acting and then see what happens. Life energy will become the real, not ego energy, and then you will feel things changing in response to the effect you have created... spontaneously.

So, how to get out of the head with all its conditioning for misery? Only one thing is possible: don't create any fight inside and don't create any effort to come out. Every effort will reinforce the conditioning. Simply watch. Don't try to get out. If you can watch, in those moments of watchfulness there will be no head to be out of. Suddenly you will be *beyond*. Not out... beyond. Suddenly you will be hovering beyond yourself.

Truth be told, you are already beyond! You have *never* been "in." The *feeling* that you are "in" is just a false conception, a produce of conditioning to be miserable. Thoughts are there, "in," but you are not "in." The watcher is always beyond. The watcher can *never* be "in."

You can call it witnessing, awareness, mindfulness, or whatsoever you choose to call it. But the secret is: watch!! Watch. And, when watching, don't judge. If you judge, watching is lost. Don't evaluate. If you evaluate, watching is lost. Don't comment. If you comment, you have missed the point. While watching, just watch... a river flowing. Watching the river, suddenly you will be beyond. Then you can move on this earth without a head.

The head belongs to the body, not to *you*. To get into the head, and then get caught into it, and then to make efforts to come out is a formula for making your whole life chaos. Once you know that by watching you are beyond, you become *headless*. Then you move on this earth without any head. Your physical head will be there, but the involvement, the obsession, is not there. What a beautiful phenomenon! A man moving without a head. Again, that is what I mean when I say become a white cloud, a headless phenomenon.

The secret is total absorption wherever it happens. For five hundred years after Buddha, his statue was not created, his picture was not painted. Whenever a Buddhist temple was created, only the picture of the Bodhi tree was there. That was beautiful, because in that moment when Siddhartha became Buddha, he was not there, only the tree was there. He had disappeared for the moment.

Find moments when you are not. Those will be the moments when you will *be*. My whole teaching is simply this: whatsoever you are, accept it totally so nothing is left out to be achieved. The mind lives on distinctions, on divisions. Don't allow these divisions. Accept whatever is, and accept without any analysis. Accept totally. Acceptance is prayer.

## Allowing Mystery is the Secret

I offer this advice for those who seek to solve life's mystery: Life is not a problem demanding a solution from you. You cannot solve this mystery—you can *become* it. You cannot do anything about the mystery, but you can do something about *you*. You can become *more* mysterious. Then the similar can meet with the similar, the same can meet with the same. You can be one with the mystery... merged. Then ecstasy arises, then bliss—then the ultimate that can happen to a being, the ultimate Joy.

Why do we want to know the cause? Why do we want to go deep into a thing and come to the very base of it? Because if you know every why, if you know every answer about a thing, you have become the master of it. Then the thing can be manipulated. Then the thing is not a mystery; there is no awe, no wonder about it. You have known it—you have killed its mystery.

When the mind is at ease because it thinks it knows, a mystery has been lost. The mind is a killer, a murderer, the murderer of mysteries. The mind is always at ease with anything dead. With anything alive, mind feels uneasy—because it cannot be the total master. There, in mystery, living is always there—unpredictable.

Mystery makes you uneasy because it is something greater than you, something which you cannot manipulate, and something which you cannot use as a thing. Mystery is something which overwhelms, something which overpowers, something before which you are naked and impotent—something before which you simply dissolve.

Whenever ego is not fed, uneasiness and discomfort are felt. So there are two ways to be at ease. One is to go on feeding the ego, another is simply to drop it. And remember: the first way is temporary. The more you feed the ego, the more it demands, and there is no end to it.

If instead the feeling of mystery is retained, then every answer leads you into a deeper mystery. Then the whole thing becomes qualitatively different. Then you ask, not to get an explanation, but to get *deeper* into the mystery. Then curiosity is not mental, then it becomes enquiry—a deep enquiry of being. When a wise man says, "I don't know," he is not hankering after knowledge, he is simply stating a fact. When you can say, with your total heart, "I don't know;" in that *very* moment, your eyes become open. The doors of *knowing* are open.

Allowing is the secret of all secrets. If you can realize this, much more will immediately become possible. You will be more open, less closed, more vulnerable, more receptive. Then life can pass through you. Then life becomes just a breeze, and you become an empty room. Life comes and goes, and you allow it. When you are empty, when just a vacuum exists, meeting happens. Anybody who is capable of being empty will merge. This is the only way to become one with existence. You may call it love, you may call it prayer or meditation or whatsoever you like.

One-tenth of your being is known to you, nine-tenths is just in darkness. For certain purposes, you may take yourself as an individual—but in reality it is not so. Your boundaries are meeting with everyone else's. And not only with human beings—with trees, with rocks, with sky... with everything. Boundaries are fictions, hence separate individuals are fictitious. Live is not divided. We are not like islands, we are one. The oneness has to be felt. Once you feel this oneness, time disappears, space becomes meaningless. Suddenly you are transported from both time and space. Then you are—simply you *are*. Then this moment becomes the eternity. The whole time process is just a long extended now. The whole of space is just expanded here.

Your consciousness should be the target. The crescendo is reached with the individual being. The climax is reached, but it is always reached with a consciousness, not with a collective unconscious. To reach it, just remain mysterious. That means not searching for anything, not seeking any achievement. Just living moment-to-moment, drifting—drifting like a white cloud.

To be mysterious in this simple way is a very uncommon quality. To be mysterious is rare; to be absolutely mysterious is really extraordinary. Become mysterious, and then you become extraordinary. No other delight has ever been known, no other delight is there: the delight of *total* disappearance!

You have a need to be needed. When more and more people need you, you feel better and better. You want to be occupied. That's why you cannot drop the ego. Unless you are ready to be empty, unoccupied, unless you are ready to be nobody, unless you are ready to enjoy and celebrate life *even* if you are not needed, ego cannot be dropped. If you can remain unoccupied, if you can remain satisfied without being needed, the ego can drop this very moment. But these "ifs" are big.

## Ripening then Dropping the Ego

Ego is a survival mechanism. The child grows through the growth of the ego. But that does not mean that you have to remain with it forever. It is a natural growth *and then* there is a second step when it has to be dropped. That too is natural. But the second step can be taken only when the first has come to its crescendo, its climax, when the first has reached its peak. If you simply allow it to grow and help it to grow, there will be *no* need to drop it. Then ego will drop of its own accord.

Before you can lose your ego, you must attain it. Only a ripe ego falls to the ground. This is something basic to be understood: the ego must come to a peak, it must be strong, it must have attained an integrity—only then can you dissolve it. A weak ego cannot be dissolved. When your ego comes to its peak, then you will not need a Buddha or me to tell you that the ego is hell. You *will* know it—because the peak of the ego will be the peak of your hellish experience. And then there is not a need for anybody to tell you: Drop it! It will be difficult to carry it on.

It is like this: you are a dream. If the dream comes to a peak, it will be broken. Always it happens—whenever a dream comes to a climax, it is broken. And what is the climax of a dream? The climax of a dream is the feeling that it is "real." You feel this is real, not a dream, and you go on and on and on, to a higher peak, and the dream becomes *almost* real. It can never become real; it becomes almost real. It comes so close to reality that now you cannot go further, because one step more and the dream will become real—and it cannot become real because it is a dream! But when it comes so close to reality, sleep is broken, the dream is shattered, and you are fully awake.

The ego is like a dream. When it becomes too close to reality, you wake up. You realize you have never been an ego. It was just a dream around you—a necessary dream.

The ego employs every type of strategy to keep you dreaming—for the ego, it is a question of life-and-death. If you come out of the dream, the ego is dead. So it will deceive you continuously. And the ego is a perfect rationalist. When it deceives, it gives you reasons. You cannot argue with it. If you try to argue, you will be defeated. Only when the ego is sufficiently ripened and ready to drop, trust, faith, and deep understanding will gain sufficient strength and transcend reason. Dropping the ego happens like evaporation. It happens when you deepen your understanding.

Sitting under a tree, not thinking of past and future, just being there, where are *you*? Where is the "I"? You cannot feel it. It is not there. The ego cannot exist and has never existed in the present moment. Only when you become unreal, then you live in the future: you make up dreams and pursue them until you gain them. That is the ego at work. The ego is the collectivity of all your dreams, of all that is unreal, and of all the attempts to make the unreal seem real. That aspect of you that is a hope-creating mechanism is the ego. The ego thrives on hope: hope for a better future, hope for more meaning to your life.

If one hope is frustrated, immediately another is substituted for it. The ego wants to live and does not exist unless there is some hope out there to pursue. And I tell you: *without* any hope, life *is* real, life is authentic. With hope, it is not.

You seek egotistical journeys based on hope and the false becomes the real. The shadow of you becomes your substance. That's why it is so difficult to drop the ego, even though it is false. It's not difficult because the ego is powerful; it is not. It is difficult because you still believe in it, in the power you grant it. You are living around the ego. You are creating the whole thing out of yourself.

So I say to you: this is just a shadow and no hopeful technique will remove that shadow. Ego is an illusion that you alone are creating and can only be ended by you not creating it. In the *moment* you see that ego is just a shadow, it has been dropped already. Seeing the point, you have dropped all hopes. You have become perfectly hopeless, perfect in your hopelessness. You are enlightened.

It is a simple insight, not an outcome of years of practice or divine grace. It is a question of a direct insight, an immediate penetration into the phenomenon of what is happening, of why you hope, or why you can't be without hope. And a realization of what you have gained and what you have lost out of all your years of hoping.

See it. It drops by itself. You are not even required to drop it. That's why I say it is easy, and I know well it is very difficult. Difficult because of you, easy because of itself. The phenomenon is easy—you are difficult. So what is to be done? In fact, there is nothing to be done. You only need clearer eyes, more perceptive eyes, more penetrating eyes.

All that is needed is to have a fresh look about you, your being, whatsoever you have been doing, hoping—a fresh look. In that fresh look, in that innocent look, ego drops by itself, of its own accord. Be that look, but please don't be hopeful.

## Living with Paradox

Zen teaches effortless effort, traveling the pathless path, entering through the gateless gate. Zen always evokes the contrary term immediately, just to give you the hint that the process is going to be dialectical, not linear. The opposite is not to be denied, but absorbed; not left aside, but used. Unused, you will miss much.

Do much, but don't just be a doer. Also be a non-doer—then you achieve both. Move in the world, but don't be a part of it. Live in the world, but don't let the world live in you. Then the contradiction has been absorbed. Then you are not rejecting anything, not denying anything. Then the *whole* has been accepted, paradox and all.

Activity alone creates madness. The still point is needed to counterbalance the movement: action demands stillness, just as stillness demands action. Once you know that between the opposites, balance is possible; and once you have a glimpse of it, then you know the art of living. Then everywhere in life, in every dimension of life, you can maintain that balance very easily. You remain artful. You remain paradoxical.

This still point that counterbalances the active self is not to be created. It is there! You are not to do anything about it. It has always been there. It is your very being, the very ground of your being. It is what Hindus call the "atma," the Soul. It is there, but unless your body—your material existence—becomes totally active, you will not be aware of it. With total activity, the total *inactivity* becomes apparent. The activity gives you a contrast.

Suddenly, amid the motion, you become aware of a point which is still, absolutely still. This is the unmoving center of the whole moving world. Effort on the part of the periphery; no effort on the part of the center. Movement on the periphery, stillness at the center. Activity on the periphery, absolute inactivity at the center.

But you are not seeking this silent center as the ultimate goal. A balance has to be achieved. And balance can be achieved only when you use both the polarities. If you use one, you become dead. If you get identified with the periphery, you will only know ego and mind. If you get identified with the still point, you will know the inner self, but you will still not know God. Either you are both, center *and* periphery, or you are still lost in mind. When you are neither moving nor non-moving, this is the ultimate transcendence. The periphery is visible, the center becomes visible. You are balanced between the two and have transcended both and merged with the Invisible. This is what Hindus call *the Brahma.*

If you remain alert, you will see: first, changes of energy in the body; second, dropping of the thoughts from the mind; and third, dropping of the ego from the heart. You will have been transplanted into a new world. When you transform the energy, you have become divine. And remember, when I say "divine," both things are implied: nature and God meet in you—nature with its wild beauty, God with total grace. So doing or non-doing is not the choice. True silence always comes through alertness. Be alert, and by and by energies are transformed. The old dies and the new is born.

### The Mystery of Love

Relationship is created by you, but then, in its turn, relationship creates you. Two persons meet... that means two worlds meet. It is not a simple thing—very complex, the most complex. Each person is a world unto himself or herself—a complex mystery with a long past and with eternal future. In the beginning, only peripheries meet. But if the relationship grows intimate, becomes closer, becomes deeper, and then, by and by, the two centers start meeting. When centers meet, it is called "love."

The periphery is always old. It cannot remain new because every moment it is getting old, stale. The center is always new, always fresh and young. The center is the soul and your soul is neither a child nor a young person nor an old adult. Your soul is simply eternally fresh. It has no age. Once you are in contact with it, love is an every-moment opportunity. Then the honeymoon never ends. Centers open; boundaries merge.

Love is actually very rare. To meet a person at his or her center is to pass through a revolution yourself, because if you want to meet a person at *his* or *her* center, you will have to allow that person to reach to your center also. You will have to become vulnerable, absolutely vulnerable and open. This requires that you are not afraid, not fearful of such intimacy. Fear-oriented living can never lead you into deep relationship. You remain on guard, and the other cannot be allowed to penetrate you to your *very* core. Up to an extent you allow the other, and then the wall comes and everything stops. A fear-oriented partner is always calculating, planning, arranging, safeguarding. His or her whole life is lost in this way. In contrast, the love-oriented partner is not afraid of the future. That person lives here and now.

Love is the natural religion. Anything else introduces some elements that are unnatural. It is not an easy religion to follow, since your ego will fight you at every turn. Still, if you take love as the basis of your spiritual practice, as inner discipline, and bring your total energies to relationships, you will destroy your ego's grip. And destruction of the ego's grip is the point, the goal. Ego is a disease if you are unconscious about it; ego is a game if you are conscious about it. You can enjoy ego, you can play it. But be a conscious, a mindful lover.

To practice love in this way, think as if there is no past and think as if there is no future. This moment is all that is given to you. Work it out—as if this moment is the all. Ask: how can you transform your energies into a loving phenomenon this very moment? Compassion, love, activity, or whatsoever the dimension, the same rule applies: whatsoever you want to *be* more, *do* the same. If you want to become an infinite source of love, then go on sharing love as much as you can. Don't be a miser—only misers lose energy. Love more and you will have more love to give. Become a miser and think: "If I love more, then my love will be dissipated and sooner or later I will not have any love any more to give;" then your love will die and you will not be able to love. Use more, give more, and you have more.

If you are always giving—and give from the center—then God replenishes. So live as the ocean, not as a small wave always afraid of disappearing. Be oceanic! Never think of losing, about anything. You are not an individual, you only appear as one. The Whole is joined to you, you are just a face of that Whole, just a way that the Whole happens. So enjoy, celebrate, love, be active, and always be a giver. To give so totally that you never think of retaining or holding anything is the only real prayer. To give is to pray. To give is to love. To give is to surrender to the moment.

Surrendering means you are no more. Surrendering means the ego has been dropped. Surrendering means now the center has been dispersed—you exist, but without a center. And if there is no center, there is nothing to protect. The walls drop by themselves. If there is no one, your whole structure of defense disappears by and by, it becomes futile. You become an open space. This open space will do everything, this openness will do everything. Surrendered, you become open to the divine forces. God can move through you, in and out. Everything happens spontaneously after that. The problem is surrendering. After surrendering, there is no problem.

And now you can laugh at yourself and the world, because you realize that you could have awakened *any* moment. You could have become enlightened, you could have come out of your dreaming at any moment in any life.

### Those Who Peak

One of the deepest psychologists in the West, of the 20th century, was Abraham Maslow. Throughout his whole life, he worked around the phenomenon of "peak experience." Trying to probe into this phenomenon—the peak, the ultimate, the enlightenment of Buddha, the ecstasy of Boehme and Eckhart—Maslow became aware of two types of people. One were those who had peak experiences and the other were those who did not have these experiences—who did not peak.

Those who peak are ready and open and receptive; those who do not peak are convinced that no peak experience is possible. The latter create walls around themselves, and because of those walls they cannot have any ecstasy. When they cannot have any ecstasy, their original standpoint is confirmed. In contrast, those who peak don't argue with their mind. They simply allow things to happen. And then, even in ordinary life, sometimes, certain ecstatic peaks are achieved.

What do those who peak have? How do they structure their minds so they are open? Here is their formula: Less reason, more trust; less practicality, more adventure; less prose, more poetry. In short, to be like them, you have to stop depending on logic—otherwise, divine happiness is not for you.

Logic is suicidal. For those who peak, logic is recognized as a tool of those who refuse to soar. Logic will prove that life is misery. Logic will prove that there is no meaning. Logic will prove that there is no God. Logic will prove that there is no possibility of any ecstasy. Logic will prove that life is just an accident, and in this accidental life, you must manage somehow to exist and get by. That kind of life is not nearly enough for those who peak.

Those who peak have learned to surrender. Their lives have become more intense. Every step says to them: "Go beyond it, much more is hidden beyond and can be discovered." *Beyond* becomes the goal—transcend wherever you are and go beyond. For them, life has become an adventure, continuous discovery within the unknown. It is existential, not intellectual—it is total. It is a question of responding with the whole being.

When you are not forcing, but floating like a white cloud, just roaming and peaking, not making any effort to reach anywhere... there is no goal, no effort. When you don't do anything, the ego cannot exist. In a non-doing moment, the ego disappears. Looking at the sun rising, looking at a flower opening, looking at the moon shimmering in a cold lake, not doing anything—suddenly, Spirit will descend on you. You will find the whole existence is filled with the divine, your every breath is divine.

Nobody else can travel your path. It cannot be borrowed. When you have had enough effort, reach to effortlessness. When you have had enough seeking, reach to non-seeking. With mind, arrive at no-mind.

# 6
# Martin Buber

*Martin Buber was born in Vienna in 1878. He was an ardent Zionist and played a major role in the revival of Hasidism, the mystical movement that swept East European Jewry in the eighteenth and nineteenth century. He spoke and wrote elegantly regarding community, educational reform, and man's relation to God. He taught philosophy from 1938 to 1951 at the Hebrew University of Jerusalem. He died in 1965. The materials included here were extracted from his classic work, I and Thou (New York: A Touchstone Book, 1970), originally written in 1923 in German. The editing here was more intrusive than with the other materials in this collection, but great effort was made to retain Buber's tone and intent.*[1]

## Our Essential Twofold Choice

The world is twofold for humans in accordance with the twofold choice always before you. You may choose to engage the world from a psychological distance through an ↓I-it↓ experience. Or, you may choose to enter intimately into ↑I-Thou↑ relation. The world of each of us is always encountered through one or the other of these essential pairs *and* always as a result of a choice we make. There is no ↓it↓ that stands apart from its paired ↓I↓ and no ↓I↓ that stands apart from some ↓it↓. Similarly, there is no ↑*Thou*↑ nor ↑I↑ that exists apart from ↑I-Thou↑.

The psychological world, as typically experienced, belong to ↓I-it↓. ↓I↓ perceives something. ↓I↓ feels something. ↓I↓ imagines something. ↓I↓ wants something. ↓I↓ senses something. ↓I↓ thinks something. All these experiences and their like are the basis of the realm of ↓I-it↓.

However, human life does not consist merely of all these and their like. The realm of ↑I-Thou↑ has an entirely other basis. Whenever you abandon ↓I-it↓ experience to meet ↑Thou↑, you no

[1] The convention of using downward and upward pointing arrows to clearly denote and set apart the two choices and the mindset associated with each was the invention of the editor and not Buber. For maximum effect, when you encounter a pair of downward arrows feel yourself sinking; and when you encounter a pair of upward arrows experience yourself soaring.

longer engages a something or someone; you do not objectify that person or thing. Instead you as ↑I↑ stand in relation with them... and, in so relating to ↑Thou↑, you also stand in relation to God, the ↑Eternal Thou↑. Hence, ↑I-Thou↑ relations are more completely and accurately indicated and experienced as ↑I-Thou-God↑ relations.

There is always the choice. A tree presents itself. You can accept ↓it↓ as a picture. You can assign ↓it↓ to a species. You can reduce ↓it↓ to an object and count ↓it↓ as one among many. You can externalize ↓it↓. Throughout such ↓I-it↓ encounters, the tree remains *your* object to possess and has *its* place and *its* time span, *its* kind and condition.

But what may happen, when intention and grace are joined, is that while contemplating the tree, you are drawn into a relation, and the tree instantly ceases to be ↓it↓ and you cease to be. This radical shift does not require sacrifice from you. There is nothing that you must not see in order to *see*, and there is no knowledge that you must forget. Rather, you as ↑I↑ now allows everything that was "tree"—picture, species, and number—to be inseparably fused within one whole. Whatever belonged to the tree is included: its mechanisms, its colors and its chemistry, its conversation with the elements and with the stars—all this in its entirety along with you.

But now, the tree is no impression, no play of imagination, no aspect of a mood. It confronts you bodily and you must deal with each other. The relation is reciprocal. Does the tree then have consciousness, similar to you own? There is no experience of that. What you as ↑I↑ encounter is neither the soul of a tree nor a dryad, but the tree *itself*.

Similarly, when you confront a human being as ↑Thou↑, then that person is no "thing" among things nor does that person consist of isolated attributes. That person is no longer ↓it↓, limited as are others, a dot in the world grid of space and time, a "someone" to be experienced and described, a loose bundle of named qualities. That person is ↑Thou↑ and fills the firmament.

The person to whom you say ↑Thou↑ is not located in a place nor reckoned time. You can place the person there for practical purposes and have to do this again and again, but immediately upon doing so, that person is no longer ↑Thou↑ and you are no longer ↑I↑. You have chosen again to be ↓I↓.

What data, then, do you experience of the ↑Thou↑? None, at all. For you do not experience ↑Thou↑ standing alone and apart. What you know of ↑Thou↑ is discovered in the wholeness of the relation. You no longer process particulars. The person to whom you say ↑Thou↑, you no longer experience as an isolable person. Instead, you stand in relation to that being in the sacredness of ↑I-Thou-God↑. Everything at that moment lives in God's Light.

This is the activity of the human being who has become *whole*: it has been called *not-doing*, for nothing particular is at work and thus no particulars of the person intrudes into the world of ↓I-it↓" The whole human being—defined by wholeness, at rest in wholeness—is active here. That person has become, together with you, an *active* whole. Only when ↓I↓ steps out of this, do you experience the person again as ↓it↓. In short, experience of ↓it↓ is remoteness from ↑Thou↑.

↑I-Thou-God↑ relations can obtain even if the one to whom you say ↑Thou↑ does not feel this same degree of intimacy and God-connection. Complete mutuality—when the intimate and holy relation is simultaneously felt by you and ↑Thou↑–is not common or insured in your life with others. It is a form of grace for which you must always be prepared but on which you can never count. Most ↑I-Thou-God↑ relations will not unfold into complete mutuality. You cannot expect this. What matters in this sphere is that you do justice—with an open mind—to the actuality and holiness that opens up before *you*.

### Full Consciousness

Hence, the real boundary for you is not between inner and outer experience, Heaven and earth, reality and illusion. The real boundary reappears in every instant of encounter as you make the choice of ↓it↓ or ↑Thou↑, between object and presence, between ↓I-it↓ and ↑I-Thou-God↑. The here-and-now—not a point which merely designates the meeting of past and future, but the actual and fulfilled moment—exists only insofar as presence, encounter, and relation exist.

Presence does not pass through space and time, but waits and endures for your response. Only as you allow ↑Thou↑ to become present does presence and holiness emerge and confront you. An object is incessantly ↓it↓, while ↑Thou↑ rises to the shore of continued existence, enchanting and inspiring.

↓I↓ of ↓I-it↓ will never encounter a ↑Thou↑ and experience the fullness of the moment. Instead, ↓I↓ is perpetually surrounded by a multitude of contents and has only a fleeting history with no presence. In other words: insofar as you make do with the things that you experience and use, you live in history, and this very moment has no actuality for you. You relate to nothing but objects and you are nothing but another object among objects. As an object, you may stand still or move about, bounce off others, and gather things around you, while lacking relation and presence.

The basic choice of ↑I-Thou↑can only be exercised with your *whole* being. The concentration and fusion into a whole being can never be accomplished by ↓I↓ in isolation and can never be accomplished without you encountering ↑Thou↑ in complete openness.

No purpose intervenes when ↑I↑ encounters ↑Thou↑. There is no greed and no anticipation of getting something out of the meeting. Every such purpose is an obstacle that blocks the encounter. Only where all intentions have disintegrated, these whole encounters—and not fragmented experiences—occur. As intention to get something out of the relationship dissolves, ↑I↑ emerges from the ↓I-it↓ dream into appearance.

These genuine encounters seldom last long; the magic that is revealed in the mystery of ↑I-Thou↑ relation again becomes a describable, analyzable, classifiable experience. Even love cannot persist in timeless relation. Love endures, but only in the alternation of actuality and latency. Every beloved ↑Thou↑ in the world is doomed by its nature—and yours—to re-enter into "thing-hood" again and again. And the lover ↑I↑, who is devoid of qualities and only present, becomes again and again "you", an aggregate of qualities, a quantum with a shape standing apart from your beloved.

In terms of your own spiritual development, the ↓I-it↓ is the chrysalis, and ↑I-Thou↑ the butterfly. Only there is no neat, linear transformation from one to the other. Instead, you live an intricately entangled series of experiences and encounters that are tortuously dual. What triggers in you the decision to be ↑I↑ comes and vanishes, relational encounters with a ↑Thou↑ take shape, and then scatter... and through these changes ↑I↑ consciousness crystallizes more and more. To be sure, for a long time, It appears only woven into the relation to a ↑Thou↑. But this back-and-forth comes closer and closer to a bursting point and, one day, the bonds are broken and you confront yourself as you would confront a ↑Thou↑. At that moment of enlightenment, you take full possession of yourself.

With maturity, in full consciousness and at rare times, ↓I-it↓ and ↑I-Thou-God↑ emerge together. These enlightened moments are immortal; none are more evanescent and yet none are experienced with more potency. They leave no content that can be preserved, but some unnamable force enters into Creation, and its radiation penetrates your ordered world and shakes it up. You have intimations of Eternity. Thus you make a quantum leap and become more prepared to leave your mark in the history of the human race: God-blessed.

It is up to you how much of the Immeasurable becomes reality. ↑I-Thou-God↑ encounters are not lined up to be mastered in some predetermined order, as some new body of knowledge. They have no time-space association with each other, but each encounter guarantees an intimate and holy association with the world as one whole: a world that always appears new each time it is encountered through ↑I-Thou-God↑. It lacks density, for everything in it permeates everything else. It lacks duration: cling to it and it vanishes. It cannot be surveyed; try to survey it, and it is lost. It does not stand outside, it touches your very ground of being; and if you were to say "It is the Soul of my soul," you would have not said too much. But be aware of trying to transpose it into *my* soul—that way the encounter is instantly severed.

True, you cannot live in pure Presence—it would consume you. And since you must return into the ↓I-it↓ world again and again, why not just stay there? In the pure history of ↓I-it↓ you can live an orderly and purposeful life. You can fill every moment with experiencing and using. But in all the seriousness of Truth: whoever lives only this orderly life is not *fully-human*. It is your birthright and destiny to soar. You can take pride in being an accomplished ↓I↓ and be seen as a respectable and even admired ↓it↓. But at what loss to you and to the world?

### Encounters with Destiny

Free are those persons who believe in the actual, which is to say: they are drawn to the ↑I-Thou-God↑ relation. They believe in their destiny and also that the world needs them. Their destiny awaits them as a calling. They must proceed toward it without knowing where it waits for them. They must go forth with their *whole* being—that much they know. They must sacrifice their little wills, which are unfree and ruled by things and drives, to the one great force that ↑I-Thou-God↑ relations bring to the fore. That force does not draw them toward things or passions, but instead redirects them toward their destiny.

Now they no longer interfere, nor do they merely allow things to happen. They listen to that which *grows*, to the way of being in the world—not to be carried away by the abstract, but rather to actualize destiny in the manner in which it, needing them, wants to be actualized by them. They believe in this destiny, but perhaps better said, they *encounter* this destiny.

They do not choose an "end" out there and then fetch the means to get them to ↓it↓. They have only and always the resolve to proceed toward this destiny. Having made this resolve, they renew it at every fork in the road. They would sooner believe that they were not really alive than believe that the great force needed their notion of ends and means to motivate It.

Spirit does not rest in ↓I↓–waiting the right time to emerge–nor in ↑I↑ that ↑I-Thou↑ relations evoke. Spirit is not like something moving inside one, but like the air in which one breathes. Spirit makes itself known in the *between-ness* that joins and unites ↑I↑ with ↑Thou↑ *and* with ↑Eternal Thou↑. You live in Spirit when you are able to respond as ↑I-Thou↑. You are able to do that when you enter into any relation in the world with your *whole* being. It is solely by virtue of your power to relate in this chosen way as ↑I↑ that you are able to live in Spirit.

## Egos and Persons

↑I↑ of ↑I-Thou↑ is different from ↓I↓ of ↓I-it↓. ↓I↓ makes its appearances as an "ego" and becomes conscious of itself as a subject available for ↓I-it↓ experiences. In contrast, ↑I↑ appears as a "person" and becomes conscious of itself as pure subjectivity, pure ↑I↑-ness.

Egos appear by setting themselves *apart* from other egos. Persons appear by entering into relation with other persons. Egos differentiate; persons associate. The purpose of setting itself apart is for the ego to be positioned to experience and to use the world... but at a distance. For Persons, the purpose is simply to relate, touching ↑I-Thou↑ and being touched, in return by a breath of Eternal life.

↑I↑ is *actual* through its participation in actuality. ↑I↑ stands in relation with a broader Being that is neither merely part of self nor merely outside of self. The more directly ↑Thou↑ is touched, the more perfect is the participation. The more perfect is the participation, the more actual ↑I↑ becomes. Where there is no participation of this kind, there is no lived actuality. ↓I↓ backs out of relation into detachment and the self-consciousness accompanying that shift. Now, the *seed* of actuality remains in ↓I↓ only as potentiality. This is the realm of ingenuous subjectivity in which ↓I↓ apprehends simultaneously its association with ↓it↓ and its detachment as ↓I↓.

The Person, in contrast with ego, becomes conscious of participating in Being, as being-with, and thus as Being. The ego says, “This is how I am.” The Person says, “I *am.*” “Know thyself,” means to the Person: know who ↑I↑ am as whole-being. To the ego it means: know myself as a separate being. By setting himself apart from others, the ego moves away from whole-being to just being ↓I↓. Genuine subjectivity can be understood only dynamically, as the vibration of ↓I↓ in its lonely truth. In genuine subjectivity, the spiritual substance of the Person matures even while experienced as ↓I↓. This is here where the desire for ever higher and more unconditional relation and for perfect participation in whole-being arises and keeps rising—even as ↓I↓ remains ignorant of this process at work.

The word “I” is the true divider of humanity. Listen to It! How dissonant ↓I↓ of the ego sounds! But how beautiful and legitimate the vivid and emphatic ↑I↑ of Socrates sounds. It is ↑I↑ of infinite conversation, of relation. That ↑I↑ was present in every possible way, available, even as Socrates stood before his judges, even in the final hour in prison. ↑I↑ of Socrates believed in the actuality of others and drew out toward them.

How beautiful and legitimate the full ↑I↑ of Goethe sounds! It is ↑I↑ of pure intercourse with nature. And how powerful, even overpowering, is Jesus’ ↑I↑-saying! For it is ↑I↑ of the unconditional relation in which Jesus called ↑Eternal Thou↑, “Father,” in such a way that he himself becomes the loving “Son.” Everyone can speak ↑Thou↑ and then become ↑I↑. Actuality abides.

### Addressing the Eternal

Extended, the lines of all ↑I-Thou↑relations intersect in ↑Eternal Thou↑. Every single ↑I-Thou↑ is a glimpse of that. Peoples through history have addressed their ↑Eternal Thou↑ by many names. When they sang of what they had thus named, they meant ↑Thou↑; and not some ↓it↓. The first myths were hymns of praise. Then the names entered into ↓it↓-language: men felt impelled more and more to think of and to talk about their ↑Eternal Thou↑ as ↓it↓. But all names of God remain hallowed, because they have been used not only to speak *of* God but also to speak *to* God.

For whoever pronounces the word "God" and really means ↑Thou↑ addresses, no matter what the concept, the true ↑Eternal Thou↑of one's life that cannot be restricted by any other and to whom one stands in a relation that includes all others. And whoever abhors the name and fancies that he is "godless," when he addresses with his whole devoted being the ↑Thou↑of his life, also he is addressing God whether he names it as such or not.

To this end, one does not have to downgrade the world of the senses as a world of appearances or illusion. There is no world of appearances, there is only the world—which, to be sure, appears twofold in accordance with our twofold attitude. Only the spell of separation needs to be broken. Nor is there any need to "go beyond" sense experience; any experience, no matter how "spiritual" can only yield us ↓it↓. Nor need we turn to a world of ideas and values—that cannot become present for us. All this is not needed.

Can one say what is needed? Not by way of prescription. No prescription can lead us to the encounter, and none leads from ↓it↓. Only the acceptance of presence is required to come into relation with God. Going forth is unteachable in the sense of prescriptions. It can only be indicated—by drawing a circle that excludes every conceivable ↓it↓. Then the one thing needed becomes visible: the *total* acceptance of what is encountered.

What is given up is not ↑I↑as many mystics suppose: ↑I↑ is indispensable for any authentic relationship, including the highest, which always presupposes ↑I-Thou↑. What has to be given up is not ↑I↑ but that false ↓I↓-drive for self-affirmation which impels one to flee from the un-reliable, un-solid, un-lasting, un-predictable, and hence dangerous world of relation into the apparent safety of possessing things.

For those who enter into the absolute relation with God, nothing particular retains any importance—neither things nor beings, neither earth nor heaven—but every-thing is included in the relation. For entering the pure relation involves seeing everything in ↑Thou↑; not renouncing the world, but placing it upon its proper ground. Looking away from the world to some heavenly place is no help toward God; staring at the world is no help either; but whoever beholds the world in God stands in God's presence. "World here, God there"—that is ↓it↓-talk. But leaving out nothing, leaving nothing behind, to comprehend all the world in comprehending ↑Thou↑, giving the world its due and truth, to have nothing besides God but to grasp everything in God, that is perfect relation.

One does not find God if one remains in the world; one does not find God if one leaves the world. Whoever goes forth to one's ↑Thou↑ with one's whole being and carries to ↑Thou↑ all the being of the world, finds God whom one cannot seek. Of course, God is "the wholly other"; but God is also the wholly same: the wholly presence. Of course, God is the *mysterium tremendum* that appears and overwhelms; but God is also the mystery of the obvious that is closer to each of us than our own ↑I↑.

There is no God-seeking because there is no place where one cannot find God. It is a finding without seeking; a discovery of what is most original and the origin. The ↑Thou↑-sense that cannot be satiated until it finds the ↑Eternal-Thou↑ has sensed God's presence from the beginning; this presence merely had to become wholly actual out of the actuality of the consecrated life of the world.

The world is not Divine play; it is Divine fate. That there are world, humankind, the human person, you and I, has Divine meaning. Creation happens to us, burns into us, and changes us. We tremble and swoon, we submit. Creation: we participate in it, we encounter and offer ourselves to the Creator, as helpers and companions. I know nothing of a "world" and a "worldly life" that separate us from God. What is designated that way is life with an alienated ↓I-it↓ world, the world of experience and use. Whoever goes forth in truth to the world, goes forth to God.

When you step before the countenance, the world becomes wholly present to you for the first time in the fullness of the presence, illuminated by Eternity, and you can say ↑Thou↑ in one word to the Being of all beings. There is no longer any tension between world and God but only the one actuality.

You are not rid of responsibility: you have elevated that responsibility. You have dropped the painful, finite version of responsibility that burdens after limited, largely known effects. Instead you have assumed loving responsibility for the whole unexplored course of the world. Your action is not null: it is intended, it is commanded, it is needed, and it belongs to Creation. And your action is not imposed upon the world, it grows upon it as if it were non-action.

That before which we live, that in which we live, that out of which and into which we live—the Mystery—remains what It was and is. As ↑I↑, this Mystery has become present for us, and through its presence, the Mystery is recognized to us as salvation. We have gained no knowledge that might diminish or extenuate its mysteriousness. We have come close to God, but no closer to an unveiling of God's being. We have felt salvation but no "solution."

We cannot go to others with what we have received, saying, "This is what needs to be known, this is what needs to be done!" We can only go and put to the proof in action. And even this is not what we "ought to" do: rather we must—we cannot do otherwise. The Eternal source of strength flows, the Eternal touch is waiting, the Eternal voice sounds—nothing more.

The encounter with God does not come to you in order that you may henceforth separate yourself from the world and attend to God, but in order that you may prove the meaning of this encounter in action in the world. All revelation is a calling and a mission. But again and again, people shun actualization: they would rather attend to God than to the world. In doing so, they know about God as ↓it↓ and talk about or worship God as ↓it↓. They place a "divine" ↓it↓ in the realm of things. This must be avoided.

The pure relation can be built up into space-time continuity only by becoming embodied in the whole stuff of life. It cannot be preserved, but only put to the proof in action. It can only be done, poured into life. We can do justice to the relation to God only by actualizing God in the world in accordance with our ability and the measure of each day, day by day.

While each moment stands alone, continuity and duration are achieved as more beings become ↑Thou↑, as they are elevated by their ↑I↑ to ↑Thou↑, so that this holy basic word sounds through all of them. In this way alone, the passage of human life creates an abundance of actuality; and although human life cannot and ought not to overcome completely ↓it↓ experiences, life becomes so permeated by relation that the ↓I-it↓ world gains a radiant and penetrating constancy. Then, the moments of supreme encounter are no mere flashes of lightning in the dark, but are like a rising moon in a clear starry night.

# 7
# Mary-Margaret Moore

*Bartholomew was a "knowing energy" channeled for almost two decades by and through Mary-Margaret Moore. She developed the capacity to relax into the moment and let this inexplicable power build around and in her body. For the next period of time, she and this energy were one and Bartholomew spoke. As she explained, it was not a trance or a sense of being "taken over." Instead, "there was an exhilarating sense of vastness, limitlessness, boundlessness in the moment. Then the words come, who can say from where or how. It was not me. It just happened." The materials presented here were extracted and gently edited from* Journeys with a Brother: Japan to India *(High Mesa Press, 1995).*

## Let's Do it!

The intention here is to awaken you to the continuous flow of awareness that is always present, to allow you to relax into the present moment sufficiently to be able to let go into the fullness of enlightenment. And why not? *You* are the one who doesn't think you can do it. I am here to say you can and let us do it *now*. It is time to do it and get on with it, and I would like to tell you precisely what we mean by "do it."

You have been looking for God, forgetting that what you are *is* the God experience. You have decided that the life you are now living can't be it, so you name the experience something else, and then spend endless time and energy searching for that "something." In truth, *this is it! Your experience as you are experiencing it now is IT.* You miss it by denying the reality of this statement.

You like to believe the God experience can't be your irritation, or your boredom, or your judgmental response to the weather, or your worries, or your relationships. These things are also God... if you remember, on an ongoing basis, to drop into the moment and allow yourself to *feel the moment* exactly as it is without thinking about it.

Remember, the greatest obstacle to your enlightenment is the belief that you are not already enlightened. You might argue that you don't want "enlightenment" if what you are experiencing now *is* enlightenment. But this is because you are missing it. You are missing the light in your own experiences. I want you to understand what this means. You are never going to feel the light by looking for it someplace "other," because it is already present in the state of what is happening right now. *What you put your awareness on is what reveals itself.* Use your awareness to help you awaken to your Self.

### This Moment is All There Is

You cannot think yourself to God. The more time you spend in your thinking, judgmental mind, the further you distance yourself from what is happening right now! The mind is the one most constant deflector of awareness. It is true the mind is a magnificent vehicle capable of amazing things. But just as taking a bath feels wonderful and relaxing, sitting in the tub twenty-four hours a day, seven days a week is no longer an exciting event. It's the same with your thoughts.

The tyranny of your mental process takes you out of the moment. It returns you to the past, which is filled with guilt or inflated memories. It catapults you into the future filled with fantasy, expectations, and possible fears. You are caught in the middle, trapped between these two polarities, trying desperately to be happy.

It is this feeling of being caught in the middle, between past and future that you ought to be running from. But you run away with more thoughts, thus perpetuating the tyranny. The way out is to *pay attention*. Snuggle down into the moment and you can stop your relentless thinking. *You are trying to find something that is already fully, totally present.* Allow yourself to experience the simplicity of what I call "your natural being," your naturalness in the naturalness of the moment.

Being in the moment is not something you have to do. It is something you are *always doing* and cannot cease to do. But you may not be aware it is a constant, ongoing occurrence, and therein lays the difficulty. Don't struggle with how to be aware. Do not think you have to start being aware of awareness. You can't be aware of awareness, you can only *be* awareness.

You may decide what to think, but do you decide to think? Do you decide to breathe or see, or are breathing and seeing sensations you become aware of in the present spontaneous moment? There is something going on in this moment that you are responding to all the time. There is something alive that you need to learn to become aware of and begin to relax into. This moment of awareness is where you are, and this moment of awareness is all there is. It is what's happening.

Don't get fancy; stay with what is intimately surrounding you. How do you experience anything? By using what you have. You know you can hear. You know you can see. You know you can breathe. And you certainly know you can think. Stay with what you know. Don't tell yourself stories; don't make things up.

The natural self is beautifully filled with natural well-being. In the midst of any difficulty, any pain, rejection, loss, misunderstanding, confusion, or doubt, there is an absolute, ongoing constancy that those who experience it call "bliss and ecstasy." Sit in the moment, as best you can with the rat-a-tat-tat barrage of past and future hammering at you, and breathe, see and hear in the moment, as it "naturally" is. Behind all the ever-changing ego drama is that bliss, the well-being of being. There is a total, *full* state of well-being.

### Things Happen, Let Them

Once you become aware of the incredible space surrounding every idea, belief, opinion, object, or person, you will relax and allow yourself to see that the interaction with that space is more interesting and spacious than you previously imagined. There is so much more *present*. You will not mind so much if the person frowns instead of smiles. Everything both shrinks and expands to its proper perspective, two small little bodies in the midst of an immense, vast, marvelous space. It's the importance you attach to the response of this "other person" that causes you to be disturbed. When the experience of that person becomes part of a vaster reality, the focus shifts. The tension eases.

In the end, what you like and dislike in the "other," react to positively or negatively, are just ever-changing parts of the human condition. Your beliefs and attitudes rise and fall all the time. When you see that these beliefs and attitudes are less interesting than the experience of the vastness in which they rise and fall, which is *the space*, you can begin to develop a sense of humor around your ever-changing desires. You realize, without doubt, that your likes and dislikes are really unimportant in the light of your true spacious nature.

You cannot organize your life to always look the way you want it to. You cannot get the outside world to be silent. The baby will always cry. The people will always talk. The dog will always bark. Things happen. Please understand; the job is *not* to choose between the chanting monk and the crying baby. The job is to learn to allow it all to play within your field of awareness.

Actions rise and fall. Events rise and fall. Sounds rise and fall. Emotions rise and fall. Everything rises and falls in the midst of a vast "something." So pay attention. Don't get yourself stuck on whether you like or dislike what happens to be rising and falling in the particular moment, because in the next moment it will be different. When you invite it *all* in—the children, the noise, the discomforts, even the people applauding you and the people booing you—something happens. All of a sudden that wonderful open space in which things rise and fall is *experienced*, and you no longer have the tension produced by wanting everything to be a certain way. And when you finally allow all things to simply happen, the body begins to relax. It can then breathe its own breath, with its own rhythm, expansively and deeply.

### Be Kind to Your Cells

The mind gives the body messages, and the body responds. It's this body/mind combination that can bring either a feeling of well-being, love, and light *or* a feeling of tension, fear, and separation. It's up to you what message it receives. There are at least three trillion cells in the body. These three trillion cells are constantly listening for messages from your mind. While you may not be paying conscious attention, the cells are *always* listening. They hear all the repetitive trivia that goes through your mind. And they respond to what they hear by expanding or contracting.

When they hear something that makes them feel safe, they expand. When they hear something fearful, they contract. Cells are not the thinking part of the mind/body union. They are *receptive*, and their function is to await the directive of the minds. What you give as a directive is what the cells will pay attention to. So, give your cells the conscious command to relax and expand, relax and expand. Let this be a sweet, gentle mantra through all your tense moments, and the cells will begin to relax and expand in the midst of anything. When the cells relax and expand, you have more options; you are more open and alive to the moment.

Every moment of your life, you have the opportunity to bathe your cellular structure with gratitude, love, and appreciation, even when there is something in the body you do not view as perfect. No scolding the "bad" and praising the "good"—just an easy acceptance of it all, and a gentle movement toward an expansive kind of energy. Flood your body with the gift of loving nourishment clear down to the cellular level. A gift from you to you.

Do this, and you will begin to feel the incredible presence of a loving vibration deep on the cellular level. This is an experience you have been waiting for. Your mind may say, "I don't think my body is magnificent." Do not worry about what your mind thinks. I want you to let your cells hear this message, "I totally love and accept my magnificent body." Your cells are waiting like parched desert sands for the water of your approval and gratitude.

Without the cooperation of your cells, transformation is very difficult. So let's give your cells a new message, and watch what happens. Mysterious things can and do happen that your mind is not able to understand. Every moment is filled with so much more mystery than the limited faculty of your thinking can grasp.

With this gift that you give yourself, you become Self-reliant, meaning reliant on your deep Self. A Self-reliant person may not be a person who knows how to get around a large and unfamiliar city, but is a person who knows how to meet one's own needs, fill one's own life, and nourish one's own body.

When you energize your cells with this magnetic hum, you tend to draw people into your life who like feeling that hum. When you electromagnetically align yourself with the power of love, you begin to embody love. It "zings" in you. Other people feel the warmth and are drawn to it. They enjoy being in your presence because of the throbbing, pulsating, amazing love energy that is always in and around you. And the cells are the focus of this amazing activity.

## A New Way of Seeing

Most of you see/think. All I am asking for is seeing, without the need to think about your seeing. If you are willing to simply look with the full awareness of just *seeing*, suddenly you will see both what you are looking at and the space around it differently. Simply rest your awareness on it, and it will come to life for you in a new way, in its own *is*-ness. Not thinking about it is not indifference to it. This full awareness of it is a moment of love—a relaxed accepting of the moment, exactly as it is, without the need to change anything. You realize with the fullness of you being that, at this moment, there is only this Oneness.

Separation, then Oneness, then separation, then Oneness, then separation. This is the way the world is. Both ways of seeing the world are possible. All of a sudden, as you really look at something, a seeming miracle takes place—you awaken to a new way of *seeing*. It takes willingness and practice to do this on a frequent or sustained basis. The ego will resist, but that's all right, too.

In Zen they say, "There is a blind Buddha in the "hara" (the energy center roughly two finger-widths below the navel), so make it see." That's what we are talking about. You have to *see* in a new way, a way that *sees* life *fully*. You have to allow yourself to *see* from a place other than the limited ego, which is always postulating polarities, right and wrong, smiles and frowns, male and female, pleasure and pain.

What you are really looking for is the state in which desire and detachment can *both* be present. Usually, desire means you are moving toward something, and detachment means you are moving away from it. We need a word that embraces both and yet has neither of those connotations. It is more like a *total acceptance of everything.* What most people mean by "detachment" is a withdrawal of life force, interest, and involvement from the situation. In reality, the ones who are truly detached are *so totally present* that all of their interest and attention is readily available.

Detachment is the gift of the great gurus, the great teachers. They are unconcerned with the next moment because it holds no fear for them. They can be totally *present* with you and the situation just as it is, with no separation. Instead of saying they are detached, you can say they are *engaged.* What they are detached from are the results of the engagement. So instead of the usual sense of detachment, meaning withdrawal, we would like to encourage you to be more *present.*

Let's go back to the blind Buddha within each of you. The goal is to make the Buddha *see*, to see things as they really are. Then, there is no need to change them, weigh them, or analyze them. Love dwells in the midst of that kind of clear, present acceptance. The awakened Buddha says, "I will be joyfully present this moment, with whatever persona you are manifesting now, whether you love or hate me. Being with your being is enough."

### Enter Space

You stay in your small mind because you believe it is your mind that controls your happiness and peace. You stay in your small mind because you fear that, unless you do, you will be out of control, mindless, and your life will fall apart. But you can fall out of your mind again and again, moment after moment, without losing your life or your sanity. You can fall into the space all around you. Fall into simple hearing and simple seeing.

Fall out of the old mental patterns and still be here. Get *out* of your mind; don't lose your mind! No one ever ceases to think. The great enlightened ones still think, but there are long spaces of what I would call "mysteries" in-between their thoughts. When thinking needs to happen, it does; if not needed, it doesn't. There is an open awareness to what is present, and then, if thought is appropriate, a thought arises.

There will be a time when the two fields, thought and *spacious* awareness, will reverse themselves. Space will be the predominant vibrating awareness, and the forms within the space will be secondary. Now it's the opposite. Now you are focused on the forms and spaces are secondary. You have to allow your awareness to open itself out to the total space. If you keep at it, it will work. You will become aware of vast space and will also be aware of the forms moving within that space. You will enjoy each spacious moment just as it is in all its fullness of being.

Use *heart* words, not mind words. When you enter that space, willing to speak from your heart, and the other person does the same, you will find each other saying surprising and illuminating things. These words will have a spaciousness and an intimacy that matters more than their content. It is this newly found *awareness* being experienced and shared that counts.

When you present only your interpretation of the events or "just the facts," and the other persons present only theirs, you cannot blend them because you are never going to fully agree on these facts and interpretations. The points of view will always be somewhat different. So, do not focus on these. Be willing to listen to what lies behind and beyond them. Simply let go of "I'm right!" and present your deepest feelings, your deepest awareness, and then *see* what happens.

Spontaneous awakenings can take place, not only in the body but also in the mind. You can have awakenings where the mind literally *opens*, and the confusion of the brain disappears. Clarity is experienced. You can break though some very strong illusory beliefs and really know who you are. This is awareness itself.

With that *knowing*, the mind will be filled with light and the heart with love. You will move through your life with grace, humor, lighthearted integrity, and fullness of being. You will be fearless. All kinds of events will rise and fall and you will be at ease with all of them. You will be in a state of well-being that is not dependent on others, or on the pleasant events in your life, or on certain relationships continuing.

At the same time, you will fully love those who are in your life, and you will also love everyone else fully. Your life will go on. The difference is, you will do everything from such a vast space within you that all aspects of the external world will fit into that space. You won't try to get rid of anything or add anyone. Everything in your world will be poignantly marvelous.

## There is No "Me"

Zen states, that upon close observation of the continuous person that you self-refer to as "me", you will eventually discover there is no such continuous person present. When examined closely, that which seems to be a continuous person having continuous experiences is found to be just a series of discontinuous images, responses, and thoughts that rise and fall in an ever-present, *present* moment.

These images, responses, and thoughts are like silver fish leaping out of a vast lake, flashing in the sun, and returning again to the lake. They are not connected each to the other; nor is there an overall meaning of the different movements of each fish. They just rise, flash and fall. So it is with your seemingly connected "me". It is a trick that your memory plays that makes you believe you are a continuous person.

You say, "I remember," and here comes memory to suggest you are back in the same exact place again. But in actuality, you have just created a brand new event in your mind, right here and now, which differs in many respects from the reality you had when you had the original experience. If you compare the remembrance to the original, you will find they are not the same. You have *not* re-created the same event, exactly as it occurred, and the farther away you get in time from that event, the more and more distorted that memory becomes.

So, for example, when people say they remember what happened to them when they were two, I would like to suggest what they remember has been endlessly covered over by all of the events that have happened since. You re-create the two-year-old again and again as you "remember the past," and each time you do, you have created something brand new. Hence, when you draw upon the past, you are dealing with fantasies and dreams in the present time. You are not dealing with anything any longer *true*.

Now let us apply this idea to what you take to be "me"—your so-called continuous self. Because you are not paying attention, you miss the obvious spaces between one thought of "me" and the next thought of "me." You are not aware of the open, empty "between" moments when no thought of "me" is present. Hence, "me" is not a continuous identity. What is happening is that you are bringing forward into each moment a new self-image, a new thought of "me," that resembles but is reconstructed different from memory than the one re-created a moment earlier.

In short, there is no permanent self. You are not the one continuous person you think you are. You are *not*! Yet there is something that is permanent about you. It is just not the "me". As you awaken to your true nature, you find the path to it suddenly turns *pathless*. From that point on, rules or guidelines no longer apply to tell you how to "awaken." All you can do is stay in the moment and become aware of the mysterious "I" of yourself that is always present and constant and spacious even as the "me" thoughts come and go and come and go.

In being *present*, observing the moment exactly as it *is*, a truth awakens from within that there is no continuous and separate "you" at all! There is a vast immensity of some no-thing ever present, in which experiences come and go. On close examination, you will find that no matter how hard you try, you cannot find a "you" separate from this spacious "I." Why? Because there is no separate small "you."

To resist this habituated flow of thought that keeps bringing the illusory "me" back—with appeals to the past or anticipations of the future—the solution once again is to stay in the moment. Then, what is really happening *now* (without the distortion of "me") reveals itself. What is present in the moment, which is not the past or the future, which is not the small self but which is no-thing, which is the wondrous abundance of what *is* there, reveals itself and is yours (not "you"). You do not have to get "there" or seek anywhere. You do not have to *do* anything. You simply have to be awake in what is always happening every moment.

Be fully *present*. Then you will begin to get a sense it is just one moment following another. You will know your reason for living is to enjoy each moment with its pure, natural, exciting, amazing, pulsating life. All that is really necessary to experience this innocent, childlike state is the willingness to interface in the moment with whatever is before you, just as a child does.

Give those things you don't like the same close attention as those you enjoy, and you will be surprised at what might happen. I am asking you to awaken out of joy because it is so delightful! Do it, not for any great cosmic reason, but because it's going to feel wonder-filled.

### Your Connection to the Divine

You must face yourself with honesty. What is your motive for seeking "enlightenment?" It should not be to feed your ego by showing yourself and others how wonderful you are. Nor should it be to end the discomfort or pain of others, or to solve the world's problems. Certainly, you want to help, because you perceive much unhappiness, but you cannot while you are also unhappy. You cannot give something you do not have yourself.

Yes, a part of you is tired of being confused, isolated, and ignorant, not knowing what's *really* going on in your own life. But I ask you to look deeper. Your motive is an essential factor in moving you from seeker to *finder*. You must seek enlightenment for its own sake, not for what it can "do for you" or "give to you." I want you to be "vulnerable" in the deepest sense of allowing yourselves to be open to the Unknown—to the power and mystery of something exquisitely different and non-mental.

Let appreciation for the moment pour out of you. Let it rest on every flower, every person, and every attractive and unattractive or painful thing that you come in contract with. Make no distinctions. Appreciate it all. Be open to it all. You can do this because, seen with the eyes of deep appreciation, everything *is* beautiful. You don't have to do anything. Be *present*, be open, and be willing to allow the energies to change you. Leave the rest to God. You are in good Hands.

The realization of your connection to the Divine, what some call "bliss," is inevitable. It is your destiny! You are currently miserable and don't want to acknowledge it, so you do your best to find things to distract you. The deepest misery all humankind share is the feeling of "separation" from God. Great awakenings happen when people can no longer distract themselves from this knowledge. Bliss is the experience of your true nature. It is love; it is knowing you are not separate.

You and God together are creating something wondrous that has as its basic thrust the full knowledge of the God-Self. Life is a creative process, and as you awaken, there is a greater and deeper *knowing* awaiting you. You move to greater potentials, allowing yourself to risk, to relax, to become more loving and aware. That movement takes you to new crossing points where the next potential lies. The grid of potentials available to you is vast, and it always holds the possibility for full enlightenment. This "ever-present possibility" of realizing the God-within could be called "God's Grace," and is always present as a potential for all humankind.

God is undifferentiated potentiality; a potentiality filled with limitless possibilities, including limitless, undifferentiated thought, where you create a space for inspiration to arise. This potentiality moves through all the various *chakras* (energy centers through which awareness unfolds) in the human body.

We can say you are connected to all levels of awareness because the body itself, in the chakra system, is connected and open to each of these levels. We refer to these chakra openings as electromagnetic grids, or joined lines of potential. You will never, until you reach full enlightenment, ever fulfill the total potentiality of your personal grid. There is always room for improvement, deepening, and creative change.

## Getting Out of Fear

You are faced with the primordial fear there may be no God, or that you are so separate from God you can't find your way back home. The manifest-world-of-form-and-thought you have taken such care to create is so incredibly powerful that you are afraid this reality of separation is somehow permanent. That is a lie, which is all I can tell you. Nothing your ego creates is permanent, and the idea of separation from God is a creation of the ego and therefore unreal.

You know, at the bottom of all fear is the fear of dying. And the fear of dying is a reflection of the fear of finding out there is nothing beyond death. You do not fear leaving one reality and moving to another. You fear you are going to leave one reality and there is *no* other! I would like to remind you in the strongest way possible that this manifest world is *not* all this is. There can never be an end to what is eternal, only to what is impermanent.

Do not try to explain any of your fears away. Do not search for what you are afraid of, or even where your fears come from. These are just mental gymnastics, avoidances, and explanations you use to try and escape them. The history of humanity reflects this mental creation of worlds within worlds, and then the running from what you have created. Please be responsible for simply and naturally being aware each moment. Have as much humor about your fears as you can. Keep your projections to a minimum. If you catch yourself in a projection, acknowledge it as yours. Laugh about it.

As people begin to feel the increase of these fears and the discomfort they cause, many are awakening to the possibility of going within, the only place where release from their fears can be found. Eventually everyone will realize there is only one way "out," and that is "in." You cannot use your mind to get out of fear.

All you can do is drop into the sea of *ever-present love*. In that moment you become like the fish aware of itself swimming in the sea. The sea does not increase, but the fish's awareness of what it's swimming "in" is vastly increased. Love is a constant. This planet is totally filled with love—totally, completely, and utterly.

The planet couldn't have more love in it because it is an absolute, total manifestation of light and love. Since love cannot increase or decrease, it is humanity's experience of it that expands or contracts. When you experience fear or happiness, you will eventually realize that something "other" is also present. Something far more spacious and enduring within which the momentary fear or happiness you experience is happening.

### The Spiritual Belief Pyramid

Every major religious teaching has to account for both ends of the spiritual spectrum. It has to be able to help the beginner who is just coming out of spiritual darkness (and views God as a separate Being), as well as those who feel they have been getting lighter and freer as they go along (becoming ever more God). And, finally, the teaching must point the aspirant toward the *pathless* path. This creates a "spiritual belief pyramid," reflecting the idea that you get clearer and clearer, purer and purer, as you make your way to the top. Not many religions or bodies of teaching allow you to leap directly into full awareness.

The idea of spiritual guidance at different levels has evolved over the centuries. The bottom level appeals to those beginning seekers who are looking for a comforting spiritual direction. Most people jump into the spiritual path to get away from fear, and they welcome religious rules that suggest they breathe a certain way to find peace, eat specific foods to find love, or pray a particular set of prayers to find God.

Look back at your own spiritual journey, and you will probably find a time when rules and regulations were essential. In fact, they may have kept you going because you felt you were "getting somewhere." Maybe you began to feel lighter or healthier or more peaceful, and you believed that "following the rules" had given you what you wanted. Then somewhere along the way something happened, and you no longer believed that simply following rules would get you there. And you were right.

Rules are based on doing what someone else thinks will work. At some point in your spiritual unfoldment, you must move deeper than that. Perhaps you have already experienced enough different energies to know that some of them have nothing to do with rules. You may have also experimented with drugs and seen the reality of "altered states." This certainly does not follow the rules. With different experiences comes the desire to know what the *deepest* reality is, as well as a greater trust in what that reality can truly reveal. You will want to know and feel the love of God, or experience the Light-within directly. You will begin to feel that, if you stay locked within the belief structure of spiritual rules, the consciousness you are looking for will take forever to attain.

There is a never-changing Self in which all things come and go. At age seven, twenty-seven, or eighty-seven, this mysterious awareness, this Self that sees, feels, and thinks, continues within you, through endless surface changes, yet remains always the same. You can sense the very same Self in the morning that you can before going to sleep. It is this ever-present Self-awareness that you are looking for.

The ever-changing drama of your lives will not provide the answers or direction you are looking for. Whatever has the capacity to change is *not* it. What you are looking for is something so immediate, so *ever-present*, so unchanging, and so immense, that you have missed it. I repeat, the immediacy of the vast "I," the God-Self, the Light, is so *ever-present* that you miss it!

You seek everywhere else for what has been with you all the time. What you are looking for is so obvious that you do not open your attention to it. Instead, you turn away and your interest is caught up in all the many-changing dramas of your world and the roles you play in them. You grab at these roles and say, "That's me. No, that's me." You can play this game of ever-shifting roles for lifetimes, but the essence of who you truly are stays with you *unchanged* throughout it all.

*Who* sees? *Who* thinks? *Who* is aware of all other things rising and falling within your life? The answer is the ever-*present* Self, which you know as "I" but then immediately misidentify as the small "I" of your limited mind. Your small mind does not want to believe what I have just said, but what else can you do? How many more books can you read? How many more austerities can you go through?

The austerities work beautifully at the bottom of the pyramid, but they are useless at the top, because they prescribe that what you are looking for is in the future. They suggest you have to be different than you are in order to become God-realized. That is nonsense. How can God not always be self-aware?

Following rules can take you to a certain point of focus, of calmness, of openness. It cannot take you to the place of total awakening, but only so far as to the very edge of the abyss. Then you have to jump into the void, the place where there are no rules, no paths to follow.

At the *deepest* level, the enlightened teachers are well aware of this need to leave it all behind. But they are the embodiment of a process. As such, they have to promote and practice the rules, while at the same time grasping the paradox of applying formal rules to the formless. Their job is to bring others to the abyss, and allow others to be flooded with, and submerged in, the Immensity of the power that emerges. They have to prepare than watch you jump into the unknown, leaving all rules behind... jump into the moment fully, with no ideas or imaginings or preconceived expectations.

The top of the spiritual pyramid has a basic, essential simplicity and clarity to it. There is a lot of space and lightness here. It gets heavier and denser and more and more ponderous the further down you go. The bottom of the pyramid reflects thousands of years of people making rules about other people's rules. The enlightened ones made only a few simple rules, but those who followed them made the rules more complicated. And over the centuries, things have become *very* complicated indeed.

If you are a person at the top of the pyramid, you are someone who has gone through all the given rules, and yearns only to develop your own rules. There is no way to approach God's power without following your *own* rules. These rules need to reflect a state in which you can be open-minded and open-hearted, open to grace, to God, to Truth. You want them to be rules that take you to the place where only God *is*, no matter what else is happening. That is the awareness you are looking for.

## Friends in High Places

Be grateful to those enlightened ones, like the Buddha. They looked down and said, "Hmm, it's a little lofty up here. I think we better build some stairs." So, they pitter-pattered down the ladder. These great ones did it with the knowing that one day the ladders and steps will all dissolve, and there will only be the One.

The Buddha awakened to the awareness of an energy source far vaster than what he identified as himself. He experienced the moment as limitless and endless—unbound in any way. He turned to the unseen world, and what he found was formless power that guided him to his awakening.

The Buddha was grateful for the help he received and delighted at the prospect of helping others. And so it goes, in one continuous flow. That same power is available to assist in your awakening. In the end, these energies are just friends. You have friends in high places who know things your small self does not. Buddha, Christ, Ramana, and the others are just friends, willing to help. Just like-hearted vibrations of awareness that enjoy sharing from the depth of Consciousness. Nothing fancy. No traps, no hidden agendas. The fancier you make them, the more distant they become.

What did the Buddha want? For you to experience your true-nature-as-emptiness and, in addition, to help you become *totally* loving and *totally* kind. The helpfulness of the great ones in attaining this awareness and altitude on the spiritual pyramid is ever alive and available in Buddhism, as it is in the other major religions. The same awareness that Buddha awakened to two thousand-five hundred years ago is present now. The Buddha's energy is also here to help, so please remember that help is present.

Not only the Buddha, but all the Bodhisattvas (those who have attained enlightenment and elected to return to help others do likewise) stand ready to guide you. Buddhists turn their awareness to the Buddha or their favorite Bodhisattva for help all the time. The difference between you and them is they believe when they say, "Help!" that help will come, whereas you are less confident that you will be answered. Ask for love, compassion, peace of heart, clarity of mind, and the desire to live life just as it presents itself in the midst of all the confusion and pain. These are the easiest gifts to receive because they are now, and always, a part of each moment.

**You Never Left the Source**

Pure awareness has no name, no shape or form. It is an emptiness that is absolutely pulsating with *fullness*. It is stillness that is totally alive and aware of itself. This is what you are experiencing constantly, although you are not consciously aware of it. It is the awareness that I keep pointing to, keep asking you to be willing to go back to experiencing as the source again and again.

You have never left, you cannot leave the source of what you are. So why should it be difficult to *be* what you already *are*? All the thoughts, ideas, and actions you experience are consciousness. Behind that, and always present, is the awareness out of which all consciousness arises. We are asking you to be aware of the awareness of that first unspecified, unnamed, but totally aware space out of which your consciousness arises. We are not looking for the sense of "I" as in "I am a separate being," but the "I before any separation."

As we read in Genesis and elsewhere, in the first movement of consciousness, that first separation, everything began to arise. Awareness moved into consciousness and began to create in many different realms. But that natural awareness out of which these realms all arose is still ever present in you. You are "It." No life would exist without "It!" No Creation would exist without "It!" And all Creation is filled with "It" in all its forms. The magnificence of the original awareness, before the Beginning, before any "thing" arose, is still ever present and available to you.

You are on a long journey. Just like the prodigal son, you left home and wandered for eons, pretending to leave so you could return. That's it. Simple. Now it is time to re-realize, to make real once again the knowing that you have *never* left the source; you *cannot* leave the source, because it is what you are! All of the deepest spiritual teachings point to the same thing; you have never left, so you do not need to struggle to return. In fact, the very act of struggling postpones the quiet knowing of this ever-present truth.

Ultimately, all you can do is relax and observe what is always *here*. That is why the path is simple but not easy. You must simply be aware of what is present, with no idea of what to expect. No translation into like or dislike. Whatever you see isn't It. Whatever you think isn't It. Whatever you do isn't It. Yet it is present in all of these. So what is it? Something created all this. What?

All you can do is *do* it, not practice it. You don't have to practice *being* because you are always being. You are on a *pathless* path. Continue to live your live aware there is a vibrant, silent, creative principle everywhere, ever present, and in everything. Be willing to become aware of it. Be willing to let it guide you rather than you following set ideas and rules. Trust the moment to reveal the truth of that moment. Just relax and allow it to happen. Relax and allow it to happen again and again and again until you know what each moment *really* contains, passed any idea, thought, or form.

It is so simple you miss it. It is so obvious, it is so what you are, it is so constantly happening that you miss it! When you wake up, you will realize you are in a sea of enlightened ones, which includes everyone here. Everyone is enlightened. You all have as much awareness as any one of God's creations has ever had or ever will have. You have as much potential as anyone, so do not let hopelessness or frustration overwhelm you. Just stay with the process. Don't worry. Nobody is getting away from anybody until everyone knows there is only the One.

### Far More to Come

Many people are less than enthusiastic about awakening to their enlightenment. They are afraid it is going to be boring. But look at the Dalai Lama. Does he look bored? This man is having a wonderful time traveling around the world, praying and meditating, talking and laughing with people, and spreading peace and unity wherever he goes. He deeply knows all of it is an illusory play that rises and falls in the whole of what he would call Buddha-Mind, what I call the space of awareness. It rises and falls, containing within it what he refers to as the "clear light" and what I call the "essence."

The clear light is without personification, without preference, without judgment. After all, how much can you say about clear light? It has no form, shape, or color and is always simple, presently clear. That is the highest teaching in the spiritual pyramid. The essence, that which was present *before* form and consciousness arose, was the clear light. If you can go about your day looking for the clear light within yourself, within everyone else, within everything else, and in everything around you, you *will* awaken to its reality. The form does not matter, because it is the clear light doing it all.

The Dalai Lama reminds us that loving kindness and a loving approach simply happen to work better for you. He does not say to be kind because you are bad if you are not. He wants you to be kind because if you are kind, you will be happier. You will have a succession of happy, exciting, dynamic, open moments because you are being kind. Drop the drama, and open to loving kindness. Even if it is momentary and the resentment, the anger, the fears rise again, the results will be worth it.

Loving kindness is a feeling of gentle helpfulness that rises up out of your being and gives rise to loving action. You perform loving actions because they *feel* good. Be kind because you want to be happy, and you will find your happiness increases as you increase your loving kindness. It is not something you create; it is already there. It is what you *are*, not what you become.

And as you practice loving kindness towards others, practice loving kindness toward yourself. When you say, "I love myself," you can feel a response because there is an essence, a power, a substance, a light, in your physical body waiting to be kindled. Each time you say, "I love myself," and are willing to feel that love, you are turning up the power, flaming the flame, letting in the light.

You do not have to go outside and find the "substance" of love, because it is what you are, closer than any idea, any thought, and action. By turning your attention toward self-love, you ignite the power of your love. You are love itself, now and ever.

The *pathless* path you are on keeps changing all the time. At each crossroad, new information to guide further movement is available for whoever will listen. The journey is ongoing, endless, flexible, expansive and deepening. Enlightenment is ever exciting, ever playful, ever extending.

Do you think the Dalai Lama is finished? He has just arrived at a stage where, when he chooses to go on, he will be ready to create a new model of consciousness that is even *vaster* than what he is creating now. He and you are abundantly "going on" in multiple realities, not just "here"—creating through magnificent and wondrous potentialities. The enlightened ones happen to know this vast potentiality; you happen to have chosen to forget it.

Your job is not to be happy; it is to become *aware*. Never forget that, and, at the same time, play the drama with as much delight and openness as you can. Awaken to that ever-living, abundant awareness that thunders through all the many-changing facets of consciousness. That's all the *pathless* path is about, focusing on enlightenment enough to break through the illusion of the limited self into *full* awareness.

And have no doubt, you will find awareness... because It never left you. All I am asking is for you to allow awareness to experience awareness—not content. Be conscious only of the bliss of experiencing awareness rather than being conscious of something within awareness, like thoughts, beliefs, and emotions. I know it sounds confusing or unproductive, but just stay with it, and, as they say, "All will be revealed!"

# 8
# Franklin Merrell-Wolff

*Franklin F. Wolff (1887-1985) was an American mystic, philosopher, mathematician, and teacher, who combined an extraordinary intellect with profound mystical insight and authenticity. When it became clear to him that he must "reach beyond anything contained within the academic circles of the West" to find the answers he sought, he left a career in academia to engage in a life-long spiritual quest. Wolff's years of seeking included deep engagements within the theosophical, Sufi, and Hindu traditions, and, in the later part of his quest, Wolff was drawn to the philosophical works of the Indian sage, Shankara. Wolff wrote two books that provide a detailed record of his realizations and insights. The materials included here were extracted and gently edited from* Pathways Through to Space *(New York: Julian Press, 1973).*

### Welcome to a New World

The real end of all religion and philosophy is the attainment of *awakened* Consciousness. Call it what you will—Cosmic Consciousness, Liberation, the Kingdom of Heaven, Moksha, Transcendentalism, or Christ Consciousness—these all point to one and the same fact, be it well or poorly understood. From one point of view, it may regarded as the awakening of a *new sense*, but, if so, the difference is at least as radical as the shift from physical sensation to conscious thought. The change is so great as to form an entirely new person within the frame of the old. Awakened, that person may apparently still live here, yet in the essential sense that person is not here.

Being enlightened, the great and baffling questions that may have previously occupied thoughts are solved; the problems that underlie the great philosophical paradoxes have been resolved. The deep soul-yearning is satisfied. That person, at last, is born again; and a new "twice-born" steps into a new world.

Furthermore, the seeking of this attainment is not simply for the sake of one's own individual redemption, but for the sake of the redemption of humanity-as-a-whole. Truth be told, the persons who forget their own attainment and their own redemption in seeking the attainment and redemption of all, are following the path which is most certain to involve their own attainment and redemption as a matter of course. Hence, nothing is lost and much can be gained by being motivated to the enlightenment of all and not solely to one's personal enlightenment.

### The Enlightenment Experience

Habitually we regard the material substance of things as being most fundamentally "real," and the spaces between things as being most essentially empty and insubstantial. Metaphysics has long argued the opposite and, for a century, much of modern physics theory has also sided with this alternative view. But even though I accepted the latter intellectually, I did not perceive reality that way nor operate as though it were so. This all changed when the "ineffable transition" came.

From that day forth, I have fully accepted the presence of substantial reality where the senses report emptiness and have had a greater capacity to realize "unreality"—or merely derivative reality—in the materials experienced through the senses. I now also understand—or better stated, I now recognize—that "I am Atman, I am Self." I grasp that Nirvana is not a field or space or world that one enters and that contains one as a space might contain an object or person, but rather that "I am identical with Nirvana and always have been and always will be so." Hence, "I *am* Nirvana."

With this more transcendent view, it dawned upon me that a common mistake made during meditation practice is seeking for "something" that can be experienced. Of course, I had long known the falseness of this position theoretically, yet had failed to recognize it. Since this recognition has come, I have dropped expectation of having anything happen. Instead, with eyes open and no sense stopped in functioning—hence, no trance—I abstract the subjective moment, the "I am," from the rest of my consciousness. I place my focus on this "I am" reality. Naturally, I find what, from the materialistic point of view, is darkness and emptiness. But I realize it as absolute light and fullness and recognize that "I am THAT."

In this state, I feel an ambrosia-like quality in the breath that casts a purifying benediction over the physical body and over the whole personality. I find myself above the universe, not in the sense of leaving the physical body and being taken out in space, but in the sense of not being under the spell of the conventional concepts of space, time, and causality.

My karma seems to drop away from me as an individual responsibility. I feel intangibly, yet wonderfully, free. I sustain the universe and am not bound by it. Desires and ambitions grow perceptibly more and more shadowy. All worldly honors are without power to exalt me. Physical life alone seems undesirable. Thoughts are so abstract that there are no concepts to represent them. I seem to comprehend a veritable library of knowledge, all less concrete than the most abstract mathematics. There is so much to be made clear in thought but hardly time to give it expression.

The personality rests in a gentle glow of happiness. But while it is very gentle, it is so potent as to dull the keenest sensuous delight. Likewise the sense of world-pain is neutralized. I look, as it were, over the world, asking, "What is there of interest here? What is there worth doing?" I find but one interest: the desire that other souls should also realize this state of being that I am realizing, for in it resides the one effective key for the solving of their problems. The little tragedies of humankind leave me indifferent. I see one "root tragedy," the cause of all the rest, namely the failure of humankind to realize its destiny. I see but one solution, namely the realization of this destiny, which is Divine.

## Insights along the Way

Since that day of "ineffable transition," I have been repeatedly in the current of ambrosia. Often I turn to it with the ease of a subtle movement of thought. Sometimes it breaks out spontaneously. Thinking, reading, or talking about higher Consciousness, more often than not, will accomplish this. Sometimes I am so engrossed with the content of an idea that others, who are present, are aware of the shift before I am. I can continue the process of thinking, reading, or talking after the shift, but my thoughts assume a greater depth-quality and there is definite slowing of the rate of idea-formation. There is a necessity of stepping gently in order to avoid the breaking of a very fine balance.

The inciting occasion each time seems to be a new turn in recognition, combined with a certain creative act of the conscious mind. The moment of creative discovery is the crucial element. There is then a deepening of consciousness, a sort of retreat of the relative world, in a subtle sense, and then the quality of bliss flows over the personality. From a profound level, thought is stimulated or, perhaps more correctly, fed.

It is clear to me that life in the current of joy is not the special prerogative of a small handful of men and women. There are many who can realize themselves as one with this current and ultimately all can do so. Actually the transition is not so difficult. Yet a lot of hard work has been put forth in the wrong direction, defining the "search" in terms of complexity. As I have discovered, it is as simple as turning from the "object of" to the "subject of" any conscious act, by introducing a spontaneity and innocence that embraces both object and subject.

Perhaps the most important difficulty which has made recognition a rare event is the habitual tendency to focus on the concrete and material content of consciousness. Success in bridging to the ineffable requires precisely the opposite focus. Effective focusing of consciousness must be toward the subjective moment in the subject-object experience—toward awareness of *experiencing* rather than toward the content or analysis of the experience.

This shift in focus is easily overlooked just because of its extreme simplicity. But, almost immediately, at the moment of success, a very significant change in the meaning of the "I" begins to develop. A process of spreading out begins that culminates in a kind of spatial Self-identity. "I" become a space that extends everywhere that consciousness happens to be.

There appears, then, an "I" in two senses, which we may call the "point-I" and the "spacious-I." The "point-I" involves discreteness, separateness, difference, etc. and, as a consequence, there are possible attainments and failures to attain. This gives a certain meaning to desire-led action, resulting in all the features so common in ordinary life.

In contrast, the "spacious-I" is continuous, not-separate, not-different, etc. It stands above the need of experiencing or even enjoying. The "spacious-I" does not have to strive in anything like a competitive sense to achieve any value. In potential, the "spacious-I" is already all values, all qualities, at once; and by focusing, it makes any value whatsoever actual. It is a state of infinite completeness. It is consciousness of the "spacious-I" which is Nirvana. It is realization of the Self.

The Self does not stand within the causal sequence of space-time. Consequently, realization of the Self is never an effect of causes set up solely by actions in space and time. The latter may, through right efforts, prepare the candle, as it were; but the flame is lit through a spontaneous act of spirit. The individual ego is not lord over the universal Self. Hence, from the individual standpoint, the realization is spontaneous and thus is often called an act of grace. Stated in other terms, an awakening cannot be a matter of gradual attainment, step after step, for the infinite is never realized by progressive additions of finite manifolds. It is all a question of a new level or state being *suddenly* realized.

In contrast to formal and empirical knowledge, which can be talked about and debated endlessly, real knowledge is essentially wordless. It deals with the emergence to full consciousness of the all-knowing Self. As such, the real knowledge represents the salvation of humankind, while the egoistic kind, by itself in its finiteness, cannot enlighten us.

This all sounds like nonsense to the champion of egoistic knowledge, where subject and object—and hence, self and knowledge—forever remain distinct from one another in the spirit of "objectivity." But which of these two types of knowledge is rational and which irrational? That which is cleverly concocted from sensory data or that which is attained through grace? Based on my ineffable experiences, I would certainly say that the latter *is* the one that is truly rational and intelligible, albeit not material-focused. Of course, the sensory-based viewpoint would lead to the reverse opinion. Again, it is a question of level.

The essence of the preparation for the "recognition" is building the capacity to maintain consciousness apart from all objects. This kind of pure consciousness is present all the time surrounding the more ordinary consciousness functions that require objects to focus on. This pure consciousness can be isolated while observing the phantasmagoria of the appearing and disappearing of the objects in the stream of time... through self-analysis and self-inquiry. When awareness has learned to turn its focus upon this ever-present consciousness-beyond-its-own-object, on that which remains unaltered through all change, then the time will have come for the transition from the embodied to the radiant state. There is nothing simpler than all this, and yet there is nothing seemingly more difficult.

When the voice of the Silence speaks into the relative, physical world, its meaning can be found *between* the words rather than in the content of the words themselves. If converted to the ordinary subject-object sense of meaning, the deeper meaning might well become unintelligible. The meaning of the words per se, to a greater or lesser degree, might seem like "foolishness," as Saint Paul observed. And even when the words *do* convey a coherent meaning, it is still not that meaning which is intended.

To capture deeper meaning, the listening must be done without strained effort in the intellectual sense. The listeners must open up and allow a sort of "current" to flow into and through them, and not feel troubled as to whether they have understood anything or not of the content, at the time. In this meditative state, the listeners may feel, or deeply cognize, something, although they may be unable to say what it is. Yet, if they remain responsive, they will presently feel *filled* in a very curious but satisfying sense.

As they return to the same Fount again and again, understanding will begin to blossom in them. They will then have entered into communion on the level of a new kind of language. On this new level, they will encounter the living Presence and the Self-knowledge of those who have gone before them by the same route.

## Epilogue: A Parable

At long last, the forest lay behind me. Before me stretched a desert, bleak and empty, and beyond was a mountain, dim in the dancing haze, reaching upward, defeating all measure. I sat resting in the shade of the forest rim, the last cool stream at my feet. Deeply I drank refreshment and pondered. The journey had been long and wearisome. In the maze and the dark of the forest, I had often drifted down false lanes and often my courage had been shaken. Yet I never quite failed to try again and, now at last, the dim trails were finished. Left behind were vain and incomplete desires, inadequate ambitions, and now-stilled yearnings. Before, reaching all but endlessly, was a dreary waste, trail-less and void of sign.

It seemed I beheld the goal, dim in the distance, but, again, it seemed not there. Was this uncertain possibility worth the effort? Could anything be worth the cost already paid and still remaining to be paid? Oh, for some rest. If not the rest of victory, then at least the ending to the feeling of defeat. But, in any case, rest.

Thus, I pondered, while a new strength grew in me and my resolution was re-born. "Better onward to continue," I thought, "for else all this effort would have been for naught and in vain. It is better to complete the half-finished than give up now." So I arose, gathered my staff and compass—my sole remaining possessions from the forest adventures—and strode forward into the trail-less desert.

Before long, the forest had vanished behind me, consumed in the refracting desert haze. The mountain had likewise vanished in front of me, also consumed in the haze. All about me was the emptiness of burning waste. Onward I journeyed in this time-expanding void, unafraid, but weary of its seeming endlessness. I was alone in a stillness that was not peace. As I struggled forward, I could not help but thirst for the forest waters left behind. My tread soon became less sure. The void around me became a void within. I stopped and sank down upon a rock. Not caring to go on, my resolute gone, I accepted whatever my fate might be.

Then spoke the Voice... or was it voices? The sound came from the beyond and told of the glory there. The accents were strong, cheering, comforting. Within me, a new courage grew, a new determination. Once more I arose and moved onward, feeling ever more clearly—although not yet seeing—the presence of the ancient mountain of untellable majesty. The desert journey was all but finished.

The way grew steeper, but somehow was easier to climb. This was the first of many strange paradoxes of this world I was entering. Quickly I ascended, filled with strength that was born downward from beyond. The haze grew thin and vanished. There, before me, stretched an immeasurable largeness: height rising on height, beyond all vision. Filled anew with cheer and rich assurance, I climbed fast... until, at last, I reached that awe-ful height beyond which thought cannot reach. Here I lingered for a brief moment, extracting—from thought—its inmost core.

Then, outreaching time and space and cause, I rose to unthinkable heights beyond unthinkable heights, finding at last the ancient home—long forgotten, yet known so well. A new world was mine. The joy was untellable; the knowledge was all-consuming. Eternity stretched everywhere. A paradoxical darkness of ineffable light enveloped all. Darkness, stillness, a void... yet, at once, fullness in every sense. Deepness beyond seeing, beyond feeling, beyond thoughts. And at the innermost core: I AM.

Here, lingering, I dwelt for a season, understanding that which transcends human conceiving. Pure meaning, close-packed and every flowing, containing the contents of all libraries and much more yet untold, filled me to the brim. I then found myself descending again, down through the haze which, ever enclosing the world below, holds the mountain top at a distance from the world of outer life. From a plateau, I looked down at the world I had left behind. But gone was the desert and forest maze. In its place, a new worldly mystery spread before my eyes: seething multitudes were rushing to and fro over a far-reaching plane. They were bent over, searching the earth, grubbing here and there but never still for long. Joyless and dull, they were seeking gold and finding dross.

Among them—one here, one there—were some rare souls who stood in pause, looking upward, their eyes dim with pain, yearning, questioning, searching... not knowing, yet hungering to know. Pondering the scene below, I recalled the days when I was like them, seeking blindly for I knew not what. Despite my newly found freedom, it was clear to me that these rare souls were not different from me. I was free—yet not wholly free, I realized, so long as these others remained bound, struggling, questioning. I wondered what I might do.

Then, gazing to my side, I beheld a glorious company of divinely noble men and women. They were reaching down, in deep compassion, toward the multitudes far below. From them, I could *see* rays of light spreading out among the multitudes and enveloping those with raised, questioning eyes. And, along these beams, a familiar Call was being sent forth entreating those it reached to awaken and draw ever closer to the ancient memory. The Call declared, "You, who would share of this harvest together with other souls that have been drawn home to peace and joy, continue to seek the way in the fields below." Some responded, as I had, to the Call, hunting for the dim-felt, unseen light. They faltered, tripped, made wrong turns, drew nearer, only then to lose hope and turn away.

Again I pondered the trials that I had known. So much wasted effort, so much fruitless endeavor. I thought, "The journey does not have to be so hard. A slight adjustment here, a little turn there, and many a barrier might easily be surmounted. I shall tell of the way which at last I was able to find so that others might, in clearer light, also *see*." So I drew a chart as best I knew. And here it is for all who, wandering in the forest or desert, wish that a clearer way might be revealed.

# 9
# Julius Stulman

*Julius Stulman (1906-1997) was a highly successful businessman and major philanthropist. He was a futurist, visionary, mystic, poet, and—some would say—a prophet. Among his lifetime accomplishments, he was publisher of the interdisciplinary journal, Main Currents in Modern Thought, and a major contributor and editor of his own periodical, Fields within Fields... within Fields. He challenged outmoded ideas and sparked new thinking at every turn. From 1941 on, he dedicated much of his writing and thought to the creation and workings of a global problem-solving methodology, that he called The World Institute, which would foster the cultivation of the knowing process and its application to world issues and individual-humankind awakening. The materials included here were extracted from the unpublished manuscript, The Metamorphosis of Man, 1982.*

## The Next Stage in Evolution

I realize what I am about to share is truly difficult to comprehend and a quantum leap or two beyond conventional thought. But these ideas are not my invention or speculation. I am speaking what I *hear* and what others have heard and what others are destined to *hear*. Each of us is being guided to awaken more and more to these possibilities. As individuals yes, but simultaneously as Humankind[2], we are being urged and goaded to become increasingly more receptive to intelligence feedings... feedings that inform, condition, and prepare us for full participation in the universal creative continuum.

I must remind you that you are not an isolated creature struggling to survive and prosper among other isolated creatures. You are intimately connected to all men and women within a consciousness-wide web. When you act, the web moves. When

[2] As a pioneer in general systems thinking as well as a mystic, Stulman not only understood but actively sensed the world as fields operating within higher-order fields and, in turn, within still higher-level Fields. He aimed to convey that individuals do operate and find enlightenment as individuals, but also always integrated wholly within species-level flow and ultimately contributing simultaneously to species-level consciousness and evolution.

the web moves, you are moved. As you become ever more awakened, the entire human race evolves. As it evolves, you evolve further. My enlightenment is your gain. We are all in this one, holistic journey together.

We stand here at the peripheral point of major evolutionary transformation. Our current stage is not unlike that of the caterpillar being urged by nature into the cocoon, prior to its metamorphosis as a butterfly. But unlike the caterpillar, we are required—together—by nature to be a conscious, willing, and active participant in simultaneous individual and collective transformation.

We can't transform blindly and passively. We need to be aware of and awaken to what is taking place—in us personally and in the human race collectively—and help emerge our next developmental stage. We are reaching out toward the point where we—as individuals and as humankind—will have evolved the understanding, sensitivity, and capacities to interact consciously and holistically within the Intelligence of the universe and be a more active and aware partner in continuing creation.

We are not *isolated* beings. Were we separated individuals, we could only feel so much, go so far, and experience only so deeply. There is so much more than that in our destiny. That is why no one person can move ahead too far of the rest. Those blessed with the abilities to reach out ahead of others are compelled to feed back what they have been fed, so all of us can pulse forward *as one*.

If this chain of feed back-to-go forward is not there, there is a void. Even if some few were to grasp what we call the "future" and ride its timeless waves, they would be of no value to individual-Humankind if there are no listeners ready to *hear* what they are hearing. So some few of us cannot go "off" on our own; we must create the listeners and the listening abilities so that the feedback from timeless dimensions becomes possible for us all.

It is foolhardy, potentially painful, and possibly destructive for civilization to blindly continue on the course and pace of present, uncoordinated science-technology developments, separatist and self-serving tendencies, and narrow viewpoints. We need to bring fresh insights to our present condition and enlightened directions to our actions. We need to stop taking and taking *to have*, and instead, must focus on creating to *share*. We must begin to exercise a radically new type of spiritually-centered intelligence, one that is resonant with a guiding and goading universal Intelligence that truly pervades all things and informs our every move and thought.

We are nothing at all like we think we are. We tend to see ourselves as limited beings, as separate life forms dependent upon but at varying distances apart from each other and from all that exists within the universe. We treat ourselves and each other as isolated "singulars" responding to the slowly changing but often chaotic, tick-tock-tick-tock drama of our respective lives. Nothing could be farther from the truth.

We are fundamentally "fields" of awakening consciousness... operating within, and integrally contributing to, an awakening humankind consciousness. We feed into this broader consciousness as it, in turn, feeds back to us new opportunities for mutual growth and emergence. Through this continuous give-and-take, we are simultaneously re-creating and being re-created. In short, we are both the artist and the art product in the creative and evolutionary process of ourselves and Humankind.

We co-exist within a single, unified, ever-changing, all-embracing Intelligence movement... a creative interplay of Intelligence-driven forces weaving their magic across the known and yet unknown cosmos. We are utterly inseparable from the Intelligence processes of nature and the universe. And yet, amid this universal Intelligence, we continue to operate boastfully in the shadows produced by limiting, ego-driven mental constructs.

For example, we perceive time as real and believe light and its multiple manifestations to represent our ultimate limits. We house ourselves within the feeble echoes of a physical universe of space and time, while ignoring the beckoning of the sounds of the spheres—infinity calling. As the prophets declared, "We have eyes, but do not *see*; we have ears but do not *hear*."

Remarkably, everything in our universe, not only us but light itself, is tending toward transformation. Nothing is as finite as it presently appears. What we presently conceive as "light" is itself a changing force, interacting with other dimensions that we are yet to recognize. As we evolve further, our antennae will discern these dimensions as well as entirely new worlds waiting to be explored.

### Intelligence Feedings

The universe overflows with Intelligence. We earn for ourselves the ability to receive more fully these feedings by being whole, holistic, and meditative. This means operating from the *totality* of who we are, beyond the limitations of conscious-mind deliberations. We should be encouraged by those poets, philosophers, mystics, prophets, and seers who did and do indeed receive "wisdom resonance" from the Intelligence of the universe. Yes, we can indeed soar high, with awakening abilities to perceive the times we live in through fresh eyes... as well as catch glimpses of on-coming emergent stages, seeded within the timeless movement of creation.

I suggest we stop trying so hard to cleverly outwit ourselves with our pristine logic. In this regard, it is encouraging that the popularity for meditative practices is growing. Meditation, rightly understood, is receptivity to Intelligence feedings, enhanced as we quiet the reflections and reverberations of the over-active, conscious mind. Meditation is not an exercise separate from living. It is an attitudinal appreciation that helps us move deeply, beyond our conscious limitations, to experience wisdom. We must cultivate receptivity to this ever-oncoming flow of wisdom, which descends upon us with its wonderful elixir and helps us emerge, holistically alive, in an ecstatic state of great comprehension.

Those who are prepared, receive, to the exact degree of their readiness. Let us come alive. Let us tingle with the excitement of living at the peripheral point of creation. Let us catch unafraid the sparks of invigorating Intelligence, while willingly accepting our individual and shared responsibilities to do what is required of us to attain wholeness as individuals and as Humankind, more fully integrated within universal Intelligence. Finished are the step-by-step methods that have guided the blind, forward progress of civilization. We are ready to enter into swift-moving, quantum-jump stages of Intelligence-guided emergence. This is what is now offered to us all.

All this is imprinted in our code, although unseen to our normal conscious mind. It takes integrity as individuals and as a civilization to activate this code. Integrity helps comprehension develop within the individual and within our collective. But integrity cannot be approximated nor achieved partially. It is akin to steering a sailboat in the wind. If a person does not know how to sail, he may topple the boat. If he knows how to catch the wind, the boat will glide swiftly and smoothly toward its destination. Still, the slightest variation can flutter the sail. And so it is with integrity. The laws of the universe are exact and exacting in this regard. Each individual receives to the precise degree of preparation and readiness to receive, with integrity, from the universe and from one another. Thus, civilization advances.

We need to feel the mist of grace and experience its powers to invigorate, enrich, and levitate us beyond the gravity forces of material constructs. And a good place to start is by observing the wonder of yourself. Look at this perfect glove you call the skin of the hand, living and ever-renewing itself, meeting conditions as these arise. Look at your abilities to think, at your capacities to love and care for others, and especially at your sense of awe. All that you are and can become is derived from the Intelligence of the universe, can you accept that this is so? You must have faith in the fact that the laws of universal Intelligence do so endow us all, enhance us, and guide us.

While making these sweeping claims, it must be understood that all men and all women need not be consciously and intentionally involved in this struggle for receptivity and emergence. Even as a relatively small percentage moves in an evolutionary-favored direction, others are subliminally being prepared. At a critical point, all will pulse forward with new understanding and new abilities, reaching a position unlike that previously known to any of us... even to the most enlightened among us.

## A New Co-Leadership Requirement

We are not a fixed seed or pattern to blossom in its appointed season. We are a self-awakening, self-creating consciousness that can and must bring the next stages of evolution into being. We do not create these stages. They are there. We are guided. We are goaded. But it still depends on us and on those now willing to assume co-leadership for this emergence.

Those among us who accept the challenges and the burden that come with co-leadership must re-educate ourselves and each other in the direction of greater integrity of being. We must grasp the fullness of Life's forces as these impinge on us, individually and as Humankind. We must permit these forces to ooze forth from our very being, transforming ourselves and everything around us with excitement, with meaning.

Our souls must soar high on the notes of understanding and accomplishment. We must be true instruments of the universe, honed to the point of readiness to receive what we are fed, and need not worry about what to say or how to say it. Our mouths will open and we will speak God's words. As the prayer entreats, "Open my lips and let me sing Thy praise."

It is a new "co-leadership force" that is required to pulse us forward, not just another body of scholars or a panel of so-called experts; not just an advanced application of our science-technology, not some collection of nations joined together to "unite" mankind. It will take deep conditioning to move us forward, first operating consciously within and through the new co-leadership, then within and through the rest.

We are not talking here about the emergent abilities of a single person or a group of persons. We are talking about the genius abilities of universal Intelligence being brought to conscious awareness as the next major stage in the on-coming movement of civilization. In mystical terms, this is a time for survival not unlike the time of Noah. We are being guided to put the finishing touches on and move into the ark we have been building for some six thousand years.

In the continuum of this spiritual development, it becomes necessary for some to step forward, in their wholeness, with a set of high ethical principles to spark the conditioning of the rest. All peoples are potentially the same, part of and informed by the same all-pervading universal Intelligence for the same purpose: to reach the highest development of which Humankind is capable.

Differences among individuals, in this regard, are rooted in their respective conditioning and preparation to become aware of their interrelationship with universal Intelligence. When it rains, it rains equally on everyone in the area. The sun does not discriminate between one seed and another under the same exposure. Each and every person, to the *exact* degree of his preparation and conditioning, *awakens* to the laws of universal Intelligence and, in so awakening, is compelled to feed back his or her understanding to others.

We foolishly emphasize the differences among ourselves, instead of accentuating our finest, collective abilities and potentials. What any one individual can accomplish in a spiritual sense belongs to and reaches out to all individuals, to be absorbed within the total of what we are and are destined to become. Each new accomplishment, in the awakening of any individual, fields itself back to all men and women to catalyze further emergence.

The very same challenge to reach the highest potential of Humankind, to go forward in eternal processes, is resoundingly echoed in the being of each and every person. There are, of course, many at this time who will become uncomfortable or outraged at the notion that they are being influenced and goaded by the feedback from others who have developed consciously earlier than they. They will resent any person or peoples who might in any way, consciously or subliminally, be influencing them to change their ways and attitudes.

However, the future of Humankind does not rest with those who fear the emerging co-leadership, for whatever believed reason. It is in the hands of those who can see in the greatness of these leaders a reflection of their own potential greatness—recognizing there are no separate individuals really.

It is interesting that observance of the Sabbath is one of the Ten Commandments. It is not just a day of rest from labor, to relax and watch or play football. It is at a different level of importance than the six days of work and whatever is accomplished during those six days.

On the Sabbath, the individual is commanded to meditate, to condition oneself to more nearly recognize the feedings of universal Intelligence, to become ever more responsive to these urgings. All religions have meditative elements central to their practices. And all, if not explicitly than certainly in their esoteric teachings, acknowledge the ever-present forces of universal Intelligence and the ability of the *whole person* to be guided by these forces.

As we come to realize the full extent of our interconnectivity and shared destiny, we will deal with each other very differently than we do now. How can we be aggressive toward another individual once we realize the adverse effects this posture has upon our own energy fields as well as those of others? In attacking another person, we are also attacking our own fields. So there is no gain in this, no supremacy, no advantage. There is only injury to ourselves and to Humankind.

In wholeness, recognizing who we truly are, we are compelled to respond to the seeming wrongs others do by doing right. This is not an ethical position as much as it is an intelligence position. By having the proper attitude, by exhibiting concern and interest instead of hatred or jealousy, by returning good for evil—by being compassionate—we are simply exercising the integrity which comes from seeing things *whole*.

In business dealings, for example, a whole person does not retaliate against a competitor or associate who cheats or otherwise acts unethically for perceived gain. Instead, the whole person focuses on creating new conditions that benefit him together with this competitor or associate. The whole person creates new dimensions to share. In so doing, he is reaching far beyond his competitor to add value to all Humankind.

Similarly, in international affairs, wholeness must alter our entire mode of action, our values, and our concepts. So long as the world is viewed through limiting viewpoints, there will necessarily continue to be competition and conflict over what is regarded erroneously as "limited resources" and "true belief." With current levels of intelligence, national and world leaders are prone to operate through fear and suspicion of one another, with short-tempered fuses, making retaliatory gestures at those believed to have wronged their side. They may sit around peace tables and agree to mutual tying of hands, but this obviously does not constitute genuine peace. No nation can feel comfortable with tied hands, even if the so-called enemy is also tied in similar fashion. Real peace can occur only when values and perceptions are *fundamentally* changed.

What other goal and purpose might there be in life other than to attain the highest development of which we are capable? And please, be careful not to see this as some end state. The "highest" development simply implies that we are turning the keys to unlock the codes of the universe, coming alive to on-coming streams of new, exciting understandings. When this occurs, we will still be at an early stage, just beginning to touch the secrets of universal Intelligence. An incredible adventure awaits us and our conditioning to receive further.

## The Futility of Singulars

We pride ourselves on our intelligence, while remaining largely ignorant of what it is and how it operates. We erroneously equate our intelligence with the thinking process of the conscious mind. Driven by its overbearing need to be in control, the conscious mind keeps the focus on concerns and goals that it finds familiar, relying for its success upon a dexterous ability to recall, reactivate, and revitalize accumulated memories.

The conscious mind employs fact-on-fact, brick-on-brick, linear thinking to weave these memories together and give the appearance of balanced reasoning and wholeness. Operating in this fractionated, manipulative manner, control is maintained and changes take place in the conscious mind and in the fragmented and contentious world it constructs... but not within us totally.

This ability of the conscious mind to recall, engineer, and manipulate memories (and, by extension, facts and things) enables us to unwittingly live a collective lie. We deceive ourselves with the belief that we can really figure things out with the conscious mind alone, as individuals and as a society. Yet every age has seen its best and truest knowledge become obsolete and its problems escalate. This is truer today than ever before.

Despite our many advances, we are now faced with increasing possibilities for mass destruction and even total annihilation—if not from terrorists and hostile nations then from environmental and ecological disasters. The ongoing accumulation of singular facts and fractionated experiences for subsequent memory recall, what we call "learning," must be recognized as no more than an early-stage consciousness function.

Our collective dependence on the conscious mind, allowing so-called logical reasoning to dominate our values and actions, must be recognized as no more than a kindergarten for Humankind. Indeed its emphasis may have been necessary for us in our preliminary growth stages leading to the present. Now, we are challenged to continue with this development, moving into the next stage of our emergent evolution.

The universe is alive, in constant re-creative change. We together must now learn to live amid this fluidity of change. To do so, we need a radically new approach, one which constantly antiquates whatever we currently think we know. We need to actualize within ourselves—individually and collectively—a non-stop, *knowing process*, enlivened by flowing, integrative minds that comprehend rather than think and create rather than recall.

With proper conditioning, we can awaken this ability and come to appreciate—with certainty—that the Intelligence of the universe, the source of all knowing, one-and-the-same everywhere throughout the universe, is upon us constantly, feeding our *knowing* process, informing us. As we awaken whole, we become positioned in attitude to absorb universal feedings, which reach us and are integrated within every aspect of ourselves—conscious mind and more—affecting all who we are and can become.

We will continue to struggle within the limits of our conscious mind, in ignorance, until we awaken, recognizing the common ability granted equally to all of us to participate in the Creation process. To so awaken is our individual destiny and Humankind's destiny. We are constantly being encouraged and goaded by nature's impingements, individually and en masse, to become ever better prepared so that we can awaken to the field forces of universal Intelligence, pervading all things.

At subliminal levels, all of us have always been directed toward this awakening, this development, this enlightenment. Inherent within each of us is this emerging potential. It is "given," so to speak. We are being challenged to reach out to the peripheral point of our awakening consciousness, beyond the limitations and fragmentations of restricting and self-absorbed perceptions, to become whole, alive within the Intelligence processes of nature and the universe.

## The Knowing Process

A real science underlies what we take to be metaphysical concepts, such as holism, enlightenment, and insight. There are invariant spiritual laws, not dissimilar from those that govern physical processes, which determine the circumstances when someone suddenly gains a far deeper understanding than he or she previously had or even imagined. The science that will explain these laws will be found to be an exact science of process, movement, patterns, systems, fields, and quantum jumps.

Through this science, we will discover that our brain waves behave in far more intricate ways than have heretofore been appreciated and understood. We will uncover new kinds of resonance effects produced through the interactions of human and nature's forces. We will eventually earn a deep grasp for the total field interplay existing between the individual, Humankind, and the Intelligence of the universe.

As we deepen our understanding, appreciation, and receptivity to the non-stop interplay of Intelligence-driven field forces, we will drop our attachments to separateness and become whole. We will experience the *knowing* process consciously. Unlike learning which takes place bit-by-bit and builds up to a whole, the *knowing* process is always whole. It is a holographic intelligence. It infuses us with total meaning all at once.

Consider Mozart. He could instantaneously compose entire scores in his head. And he knew at once that what he composed was not only good, but God-inspired. He caught it whole. He didn't have to labor long hours, putting his compositions together with the sweat of his brow. He wrote, "When I am, as it were, *completely* myself, entirely alone, and of good cheer, it is on such occasions that my ideas flow best and most abundantly. Whence and how they come, I know not; nor can I force them. Nor do I hear in my imagination the parts successively, but I hear them, as it were, *all at once*."

How could he do this? He was consciously and comprehensively awakened to the rhythms in their harmonious interplay within the universe. He listened and was *informed*. Of course, this has been, to date, a rare happening. But what Mozart could do, I can do, and the rest of us can do as well, for we are indeed so *seeded*. We must simply condition ourselves together to allow this potential to emerge, and drop those practices and block out those factors which inhibit this emergence.

In the *knowing* process, there are no singular facts, no logical arguments, and no partial grasping of reality. Without being able to explain how we know, we simply *know* and sometimes well in advance of the science and data accumulation that first challenges and later confirms the truth of this knowing.

And it need not be simply music or poetry that is *heard*. We can be guided in all our actions, be these related to architecture, sculpture, painting, or mathematics, for these all can resonate with the rhythms of the wholeness and beauty of nature and the universe. We can be fed answers we seek, likewise, whether these occur in medicine, economics, conservation, politics, or whatsoever we are deeply involved in; for there are no isolations of disciplines. Regardless of focus, we can be fed, not by an information retrieval process, but by a *comprehension* process.

As we open up to feedings from universal Intelligence, each moment becomes a new beginning for adventuring forth renewed. If we sense a seeming end, a stopping point, a point of hesitation or confusion, it is because we have allowed ourselves to crystallize that moment and ourselves along the way. We have not sufficiently understood who we truly are at that moment and have temporarily dead-ended ourselves.

When we use words in their common-day sense and ponder over problems in their accepted, limited presentations, we are drawing upon our cleverness. This will give us answers that are digestible and communicable, but which truly do not get us very far toward ultimate answers that align with universal Intelligence. When we resolve our problems in clever ways, we completely miss the potential of deeper, comprehensive understanding.

Currently, our educational and social-political systems reward fact accumulation and abilities to weave these facts together in coherent wholes. As a result, we have become fact-accumulators and glib talkers and thinkers, substituting the expedient for the eternal and a thirst for factual knowledge for deep drinking from the wellspring of universal Intelligence. We currently find comfort and reassurance in the reward systems that honor our acts of cleverness.

Soon the content of our memory is immense and we have become almost totally fact-dependent and logic-driven, with great recall and reasoning abilities but little integrity with regard to the *knowing* process. We may have 20 or so facts and truisms to pull out in response to a given problem, and can stack them up to look like an answer, but this does not evoke anywhere near the "quality response" from us that is possible when a new alchemy is allowed in the place of cleverness. Then, a flow of one hundred or more different patterns can come into play—all at once—and produce an integrated answer without the interference of conscious deliberations and mental manipulations.

We need to re-educate ourselves, recognizing that “education” is not fact accumulation but awakening awareness. More educated and capable individuals are those more aware of the Intelligence of the universe as that Intelligence informs them. More educated and capable persons possess greater integrity of *being* than others less educated and capable.

An early step in our re-education is to refrain from taking anything into our system that we don’t fully understand, that we can’t be *whole* with, that doesn’t resonate deeply within us. We should reject it, even if habit and insecurity demand that we pay it attention. We should stop accumulating new knowledge and instead start opening ourselves to the *knowing* process.

We will continue to confuse ourselves as long as we maintain a false notion of ourselves as separate beings. Being separate, we rely on words and thought patterns which ultimately mislead us, confuse us, and deny ourselves true access to the holistic, mystical experience of life. “Mystical” has been given wrong connotations. Rightly understood, it is suggestive of a more genuine way of knowing, a comprehending that is altogether different from step-by-step conscious deliberations. If we allow ourselves to be fed from universal Intelligence all around us, then we can indeed cry “Eureka!” at every turn.

Much like the caterpillar in its pre-butterfly phase of development, we have been thinking and acting with early-stage abilities. But we are now positioned at the jump-off point for fundamental change. Simply viewed, our individual and collective information accumulation and knowledge-building represent a preparatory stage, a prerequisite for advancement to comprehensive abilities. We are now ready to move from cleverness to wisdom, as individuals and as Humankind.

## Next-Stage Technology

The generation of new ideas through deliberate sequential approaches, step upon step, has seemed necessary until now. However, we are now ready to enter a new era of awakening understanding. We have lived long enough with limited views and fragmented positions and attitudes. We are poised to understand things totally and whole, at once, as we ourselves become whole. We should humbly and respectfully raise our antennae, bringing an elixir to our souls, hearing and knowing more of what the universe wants us to hear and comprehend. We must recognize that by becoming whole, we can receive a gift from the universe, given to us in proportion to our emerging levels of conditioning to receive.

Our technology mirrors and acts as a critical catalyst in this development. Much of our technology currently reflects and stimulates linear thinking, fact accumulation and recall, and fractionated concerns. For Humankind to pulse forward, our technology must itself pulse forward. Next-stage developments must emphasize field-pattern detection and field-pattern interplay. New technologies must emerge and be placed in the hands of the world's most gifted, most enlightened, and most forward-looking men and women, where they can be applied in service to all Humankind.

These applications will serve the twofold purpose of ending hunger, poverty, illness, and ultimately those destructive divisions that place nation against nation and people against people; while instead, teaching men and women everywhere a new way of *knowing* to replace and move beyond outmoded, linear processes of thought and communication. Aided by the right type of technological output, we will no longer have to think out everything in a reductionist sense to arrive at new answers. Much of what is popularly referred to as "left brain" processing can be accomplished far better by computers than by humans. It is in the "right brain" domain, and particularly in operating from an evolved "right dominant-left subordinate" orientation, that humans shine.

Computer technology can help us organize complex data arrays in formats and patterns that evoke new insights and condition us for jump-off points; but our problem solving must ultimately go beyond these data and flow naturally out of the creative integrations of ourselves within the species, within nature, and within the sweep of civilization's flow. Remember, we live within a universal Intelligence which informs us, as we open ourselves to its feedings.

We must take chances, daring to go beyond the conditioned responses and limited approaches of our times. With a holistic viewpoint, we can strike forward, to anticipate and to adventure the quantum jump. We will find answers and the courage and creative abilities to meet new challenges as they confront us, encouraged by earlier rounds of success. We will move with vibrant confidence that comes from knowing that we are whole and being guided by an Intelligence we are learning to appreciate at deeper and still deeper levels.

## Field-Pattern Interplay

The universe operates through the intricate interplay of Intelligence-choreographed, field-pattern movements. Everything we see or feel is simply another intelligence-directed field or fields. These fields have sympathetic resonance with other fields; in other words, "like fields" attract and move as one with each other. These movements are guided by geometric, other mathematical, or perhaps aesthetic lawfulness that we are now just on the verge of understanding. There is no ending, no beginning, no stop, and no break in the continuum of these energy field interactions. There is growth and integration.

Each new stage emerging in this interplay of fields feeds back to embrace and attempt to pull forward all previous configurations and stages. This has somewhat the feel of a magnetic force that re-orients iron filings in a new direction and in a new pattern. If the new stage lacks integrity, however, this reaching back will prove ineffective and the new stage itself will wither away. No stage of growth can long endure if it does not share synchronicity with all that is. However, if the new stage is a genuine response to universal Intelligence feedings, it will have a power effect on all previous stages and awaken their advance.

Through this field interplay, the universe keeps renewing—from whole to still more inclusive whole. There are no empty spaces, no gaps in the universe that are untouched. Every space is alive with interacting, Intelligence-driven forces, seen and unseen. There is nothing "physical" to limit or block a field pattern from reaching a similar field pattern and resonating with it, even if the two are, by standard conventions of measurement, thousands of miles or even thousands of light-years away from each other. They are in continual connection through the organismic, pulsating pattern movement which exists and unites all.

In the silence of their apparent aloneness, two trees of the same species not able to touch each other in any way are in communication with one another. Cut one down and another one several hundred feet away may die. There is a field inter-relationship at play here.

If a person were brought up like Robinson Crusoe, on an isolated island, could he evolve and develop for the purposes for which we are all here? My answer is "yes." We know of artists who have isolated themselves from the rest of the world to develop their work, only to come back to the mainstream and find other artists who are doing virtually the same thing that they were inspired to do. The same holds for scientists who make seemingly independent breakthroughs at nearly the same moment. The "isolated" individual is, in fact, interrelated and integrated in the great envelope of civilization's movement. He is able to receive the same force fields that influence all Humankind.

What is essential always is to see ourselves as Intelligence-guided fields, sharing movement and change with all other fields, everywhere. We should remain ever alert for the indications that we do constantly receive, urging us toward further integration within the total, timeless, re-creative flow of the universe. Psychology and psychiatry help us go deeper into ourselves, but still largely within the confines of the known and oblivious to on-coming stages. It is only through a deep understanding of field pattern interplay that we can truly understand ourselves and grasp our developmental movement and evolutionary requirements.

It is actually impossible for a human being to be immune from any energy forces which exist anywhere, recognized or not, and not in some way to be influenced by these forces. We need to open ourselves so we can better recognize what is occurring... sensing the pulsating, orbiting field patterns in their rhythmic, Intelligence interplay. That is what mystics try to convey when they say "We are one with everything that is in the universe" or declare that "You are the world" or "I am THAT."

We are in touch with, and touched by, everything we could possibly need to continue our growth toward wholeness and conscious integration within the universe. As we so emerge, it will become ever clearer that the "future" is contained in the here-and-now, the end is contained in the beginning, and the beginning is contained in the end. It is all seeded *here*.

We are challenged to resonate within the Intelligence of the universe, while helping others to be field-sensitive and field-resonant. To meet this challenge, we must trust that there, in fact, *is* an Intelligence constantly feeding us and awakening our potential abilities to be field-interrelated participants in the re-creating, pulsing flow. We must lend ourselves fully and with integrity to this Intelligence process. By doing so, we will be more powerful individuals, but must not forget that our true power, dignity, and destiny is as Humankind.

All our current divisive activities on political, religious, economic, and environmental fronts have to be transcended so we can come together as one Humankind body and move all the variations of "I am" over to a "We-are-that-also-includes-I-am." In our continued evolution, all of us can and must leap forward as some prophets, geniuses, mystics, and spiritual giants have and are now doing.

**Intimations of What Lies Ahead**

What will life look like when Humankind comes of age? It is difficult to even begin to convey this using today's words, symbols, and images. We will have earned a fluidity of understanding and a comprehensive grasp. Our continual collective evolution will be the foremost concern of everyone. People will no longer think they have to climb over others to get anywhere. Progress will lie primarily in creating new possibilities, new dimensions, and new awakenings to share with one another.

In a timeless sense, guided by universal Intelligence processes, we will share the abilities to transform what used to be worthless matter and untapped resources into valued products benefitting all. No one will be denied what they require to live comfortably. We will have mastery of cell structures and their operative laws, and earned new understanding of health and healing.

We will look back from our age of awakening and observe how we used to be “square,” but came to recognize the need for wholeness, fluidity, and elimination of pointed corners. So we made ourselves “round” and, as we did, the “square” dissolved. In fact, we came to realize that there never was a “square” at all, we were always “round” but lived the illusion of “squared-ness.”

That illusion has driven us today, as a civilization, just short of our next take-off point. However, as we have advanced to this point, the illusory orientation has become a real danger to ourselves and no longer an aid to our further growth. In continued “squared-ness,” we have the potential to destroy us all—through misadventures and miscalculations—and a growing likelihood to do just that.

We are at a crossroad, one road leading to a potentially destructive dead-end, the second leading back to the wholeness and God-connection experienced by Adam in the Garden of Eden. Fortunately, we are seeded with the abilities to awaken together in time to make the right choice.

Will this be at an endpoint? Of course not; it will be just a beginning, an entrance into on-coming adventures beyond our abilities even to imagine. We will be rooted more consciously in Eternity, with entirely new appreciations.

Made in the USA
Charleston, SC
27 April 2014